The Exceptional Teacher's Handbook

The Exceptional Teacher's Handbook

The First-Year Special Education Teacher's Guide for Success

Carla F. Shelton • Alice B. Pollingue

CORWIN PRESS, INC.
A Sage Publications Company
Thousand Oaks, California

For information:

Corwin Press, Inc.
A Sage Publications Company
2455 Teller Road
Thousand Oaks, California 91320
E-mail: order@corwinpress.com

Sage Publications Ltd.
6 Bonhill Street
London EC2A 4PU
United Kingdom

Sage Publications India Pvt. Ltd.
M-32 Market
Greater Kailash I
New Delhi 110 048 India

Printed in the United States of America

Library of Congress Cataloging-in-Publication Data

Shelton, Carla F.
  The exceptional teacher's handbook: The first-year special education teacher's guide for success / by Carla F. Shelton and Alice B. Pollingue.
        p. cm.
Includes bibliographical references.
  ISBN 0-7619-7739-2 (cloth : alk. paper) — ISBN 0-7619-7740-6 (pbk. : alk. paper)
  1. Special education — United States — Handbooks, manuals, etc. 2. Special education teachers — United States — Handbooks, manuals, etc. 3. First year teachers—United States —Handbooks, manuals, etc. I. Pollingue, Alice B. II. Title.
  LC3969 .S36 2000
  391.9'0973 — dc21   00-008796

This book is printed on acid-free paper.

00 01 02 03 04 05 10   9   8   7   6   5   4   3   2   1

Corwin Editorial Assistant: Kylee Liegl
Production Editor: Astrid Virding
Editorial Assistant: Candice Crosetti
Typesetter: D&G Limited, LLC

The original purpose of education was to produce a thoughtful, creative, emotionally alive, unafraid man, a man willing to try to solve the problems he faces in his world. Athough he may not solve all of them, he will solve some of them. Confident that he can build on his success, he may fail for a while, but he will know that some success is possible. When the time comes and success does not come easily, he will not give up.

—William Glasser

Contents

Introduction

The Exceptional Teacher's Handbook is a comprehensive resource book designed to assist and support the special education teacher through his or her first school year and new teaching experience. The handbook supplies the first-year teacher with a step-by-step management approach designed to improve and enhance his or her skills in the areas of organization, time management, and instructional planning and implementation. The resource book contains information on critical topics such as inclusion, discipline, classroom management, transition, classroom organization and design, parent conferences, and professional development for the new special education teacher. In addition, the authors have included appendices that supply the new teacher with a wealth of miscellaneous information ranging from first aid procedures in the school setting to techniques for stress management.

The handbook's contents are sequentially arranged in order to guide the new teacher from the initial planning stage prior to the start of school to the post-planning stage of the school year. The authors provide numerous time saving checklist and miscellaneous forms that will assist the instructor in accomplishing the multitude of required tasks that are always in existence. The handbook is designed to be utilized as a quick reference; therefore, every chapter is written in an abbreviated format and can be reviewed in a matter of minutes. The chapters are structured in a manner that will provide the reader with current information on the chapter's topic and proceeded by a "How-To-Do-It" plan of action for the teacher when appropriate.

Finally, The Exceptional Teacher's Handbook can assist the first-year teacher in successfully navigating the ever-changing maze of special education. The handbook was written from a classroom teacher's perspective and supplies the reader with practical suggestions. The contents of the book can be tailored to fit the individual needs of most special education programs and provides the first-year special education teacher with the necessary framework for a successful school year. The handbook is an indispensable resource that will guide and assist the new teacher throughout the entire school year. More importantly, the text will empower the first-year special education teacher with the confidence necessary to meet the challenge of the profession.

Corwin Press would like to acknowledge the contributions of the following reviewers:

Melise Bunker
    Associate Professor
    School of Education and Behavioral Sciences
    Palm Beach Atlantic College
    West Palm Beach, FL

Gloria Campbell-Whatley
    Assistant Professor
    Dept. of Special Education
    Indiana Purdue University–Fort Wayne
    Fort Wayne, IN

Tom Fischer
    Assistant Professor
    Dept. of Special Education
    University of Wisconsin–Oshkosh
    Oshkosh, WI

Mitzie Hilton
    Resource Specialist
    Rock Springs Elementary School
    Kingsport, TN

Cindy Munson
    Special Education Teacher
    Travis Middle School
    Amarillo, TX

Joseph Straub
    Teacher
    Thomas Starr King Middle School
    Los Angeles Unified School District
    Los Angeles, CA

The authors would like to thank their families for all of their support and encouragement throughout this endeavor.

About the Authors

Carla F. Shelton, M. Ed., has eleven years of teaching experience in special and regular education. She currently is certified in the areas of specific learning disabilities, emotional/behavior disorders, mild intellectual disabilities, elementary grades (P-8), and school counseling (P-12).

Carla has taught disabled students in resource and self-contained environments and grade levels ranging from second to twelfth. The majority of her teaching experience has been in traditional public school systems. She is skilled in identifying learning and behavior problems. Carla has expertise in developing and implementing effective educational and behavioral strategies that promote and foster student success. She has experience in administering and interpreting standardized and criterion-reference tests. In addition, the author has mastered the art of collaboration with regular education teachers and staff and works effectively with families of disabled students. Finally, Carla's solid educational background and broadbase teaching experience is the foundation on which *The Exceptional Teacher's Handbook* is built.

Alice B. Pollingue, Ed. D., is a tenured assistant professor of education at Augusta State University in Augusta, Georgia. She has been teaching at the university for more than ten years. Alice received her doctorate degree from the University of Alabama.

Currently, Alice teaches special education courses to undergraduate and graduate students and is the supervising professor for the entire special education teacher training program. She develops curriculum for new special education courses offered at the university. In addition, she is a consultant for local school systems.

Alice has published articles in the *Journal of Early Education* and the *Journal of Special Education.* She is active in both local and national professional organizations. Her motivation, professionalism, knowledge, and expertise make her the perfect coauthor for *The Exceptional Teacher's Handbook.*

Carla and Alice met through the Master Teacher/Apprentice Program at Augusta State University. After many sessions of discussing the needs of first-year special education teachers, they decided to team up and write a handbook that would epitomize their shared philosophies and love for the profession.

Preparing for a Successful School Year

For most teachers, preparation is one of the essential ingredients for achieving a successful school year. For the special education teacher, preparation is the key to not only achieving a successful school year, but for surviving the year. Traditionally, the regular education teacher utilizes the preplanning time period preparing for instruction and charting out the course for the new school year. However, the special education teacher very often can be found trying to confirm his or her new class rosters, resolving transportation issues, matching regular education teachers with students in inclusive settings, creating or fine-tuning students' schedules, selecting appropriate instructional materials, and creating a class schedule that is conducive to the school's master schedule. The first-year special education teacher frequently asks the question, "Where do I begin?"

In the pages that follow, the authors provide checklists designed to guide the new teacher through the pre-planning and post-planning time periods. Historically, these periods of the school year are the most confusing and demanding for teachers new to the profession of special education. In addition, the authors include a checklist of items that should be addressed each month. The monthly teacher checklist will help the new teacher establish good work habits and time management skills. The contents of each checklist are broken down into four major categories: *Special Education Administrative Tasks, Classroom/Instructional Tasks, Non-Instructional Tasks, and Professional Development.* The authors are aware that a tremendous amount of diversity exists among special education programs. However, in light of this fact, the teacher of students with exceptionalities must accomplish certain tasks if the goal of a successful school year is to be achieved. The authors recommend that the teacher review each checklist and select the tasks that are relevant, adding additional tasks as needed to meet the individual needs of his or her program.

Pre-Planning Teacher Checklist

I. Special Education Administrative Tasks

_____ Procure current class roster from special education director or special education county or district office.

_____ Procure current Individualized Educational Programs from special education director or special education county or district office.

_____ Review all student Individualized Educational Programs and complete **Student Information form** (Form 1.1).

_____ Procure special education contact person's name and telephone number (possibly referred to as a special education coordinator).

_____ Contact school counselor and review students' schedules for the new school year.

_____ Coordinate with the school counselor and place students in regular education classes as dictated by each student's Individualized Educational Programs.

_____ Conference with teachers of students placed in inclusive settings.

_____ Complete **Classroom Modifications** (Form 1.2) and distribute to teachers of students placed in inclusive settings.

_____ Distribute students' discipline information or appropriate addendums to the school administrator.

_____ Create **Correspondence Log** (Form 1.3) to document all communications with parents, teachers, school administration, and other important sources. Correspondence logs should be kept in a three-ring binder in a convenient but secure location.

_____ Complete the **Paraprofessional's Classroom Responsibilities Checklist** (Form 1.4) and discuss the information with the paraprofessional assigned to your class. Be prepared to clarify and explain all assigned duties.

II. Classroom/Instructional Tasks

_____ Procure school systems curriculum guides for academic subjects to be taught in the special education classroom and review material thoroughly.

_____ Review each student's Individualized Educational Program and record all academic information on the **Present Levels of Performance form** (Form 1.5).

_____ Establish a classroom schedule for academic instruction and exploratory, elective, or specialty activities.

_____ Procure instructional and supporting materials.

_____ Procure lesson plan and grade book.

_____ Plan lessons and organize instructional materials.

_____ Plan emergency lesson plans and instructions. The teacher should include seating chart, class roster, and any other helpful information.

_____ Construct bulletin boards that reflect instructional units or themes.

_____ Place emergency response and exit procedures in highly visible areas:
   1. Fire drill
   2. Tornado or inclement weather drill
   3. Bomb threat
   4. Other: _____

_____ Establish and post classroom policies and procedures:
   1. Rules and consequences
   2. Grading policy
   3. Make-up work policy
   4. Daily routine/schedule

_____ Prepare parent classroom information packets to be sent home the first day of class. These packets should include all vital classroom information.

_____ Make copies of the **Student Emergency Information* form** (Form 1.6) to be distributed to students the first day of class.

III. Non-Instructional Tasks

_____ Procure or request non-instructional supplies. Utilize the **Classroom Supply Checklist (Non-Instructional)** (Forms 1.7 a-c).

_____ Inventory the contents of the classroom. Utilize the **Classroom Inventory Checklist** (Form 1.8) and record all serial numbers of major equipment and note the condition of all items listed below:
   1. Number of student desk
   2. Teacher desk
   3. Tables
   4. Chairs
   5. Book shelves
   6. File cabinets
   7. Storage cabinets
   8. Computer
   9. Computer table
   10. Overhead projector
   11. Carts
   12. Tape recorders
   13. Ear phones/head sets

---

*Require the parents of elementary and middle school students to complete the form and allow at least two days for return.

14. Televisions
15. VCR
16. Printer

_____ Procure faculty duty roster and note all assigned duties and their dates, times, and locations.

IV. Professional Development

_____ Join at least one professional organization (Chapter 10).

_____ Subscribe to at least one professional periodical (Chapter 10).

_____ Procure a schedule of conferences related to special education and make arrangements to attend at least one conference per school year.

_____ Procure a schedule of staff development for certified personnel offered through the school system.

_____ Start current special education articles notebook (make copies of all articles of special interest and place in a three-ring binder).

_____ Obtain liability insurance for educators through professional organization.

_____ Set short and long-term professional goals (see Chapter 10).

Additional Teacher Tasks

_____ _____

_____ _____

_____ _____

_____ _____

_____ _____

_____ _____

_____ _____

_____ _____

_____ _____

_____ _____

_____ _____

_____ _____

_____ _____

_____ _____

Monthly Planning Tasks Checklist

I. Special Education Administrative Tasks

_____ Review students' Individualized Educational Programs.

_____ Annotate all mastered short-term objectives on students' Individualized Educational Programs.

_____ Schedule annual review meetings for students whose Individualized Educational Program will expire within 30 days.

_____ Send **Exceptional Student Monitor Information forms** (Form 1.9) to teachers of students placed in inclusive settings.

_____ Review all monitor results and record information on the **Exceptional Student Monitor Results Summary form** (Form 1.10).

_____ Review students' behavior plans/contracts and revise as necessary. The authors provide a generic **Behavior Contract** (Form 1.11).

_____ Correspond with parents in reference to student progress in the regular and special education classroom.

II. Classroom/Instructional Tasks

_____ Complete instructional plans.

_____ Update emergency lesson plans.

_____ Procure materials to support instructional plans.

_____ Construct bulletin boards to reflect current instructional units or themes.

_____ Prepare progress reports or report cards.

III. Non-Instructional Tasks

_____ Check non-instructional supplies and replenish as necessary.

_____ Review dates for designated faculty meetings or special education meetings.

IV. Professional Development

_____ Review professional journals and copy articles of interest and place in a notebook for future reference.

_____ Select and read a book on an educational topic of interest.

_____ Attend professional conferences and staff development courses.

Additional Teacher Tasks

Post-Planning Tasks Checklist

I. Special Education Administrative Tasks

_____ Review all students' Individualized Educational Programs and ensure each IEP is current and complete.

_____ Annotate all mastered goals and objectives on each students Individualized Educational Program.

_____ All Individualized Educational Programs should be in a file folder and placed in a secured location (preferably a locking file cabinet).

_____ Send IEP folders of students being promoted to the next grade and changing schools to the new special education teacher (for example, those students who are moving up from elementary to middle school or moving up from middle school to high school).

_____ Review each student's progress in all inclusive settings and record final grade.

_____ Inform parents of students' progress in regular and special education classes.

_____ Contact school counselor and review students' schedules for the new school year. (This is especially important for high school students.)

_____ Coordinate with the school counselor and place students in regular education classes for the new school year as dictated by their updated Individualized Educational Programs.

_____ Conference with new teachers of inclusive students and address all questions and concerns.

_____ Contact special education coordinator or special education director to obtain final instructions before leaving school for the summer.

II. Classroom/Instructional Tasks

_____ Prepare and complete final grades for all special education classes.

_____ Record final grades on students' permanent record (this is usually done by the school counselor or registrar at the middle and high school level).

_____ Organize and store instructional materials.

_____ Remove and store all bulletin board materials and posters.

_____ Return all materials procured from the school media center or other faculty members.

_____ Follow school policy for closing out the school year (most schools will have a written checklist for teachers to follow before leaving for the summer).

III. Non-Instructional Tasks

_____ Complete **Classroom Supply Checklist** (non-instructional) form (Forms 1.7 a-c) for new school year. Place order before leaving for the summer.

_____ Inventory classroom contents and note all deficiencies.

_____ Complete work order for broken equipment or classroom deficiencies.

_____ Review all serial numbers of major equipment.

_____ Unplug all equipment in the room.

_____ Cover all computer equipment.

_____ Store audio and visual equipment.

_____ Place request for additional major end items.

_____ Organize teacher's desk and miscellaneous materials.

_____ Clean desks, chairs, and tables.

IV. Professional Development

_____ Register for summer staff development or college courses for recertification.

_____ Attend summer conferences or seminars relating to special education.

_____ File all conference and article information.

Additional Teacher Tasks

_____ _____

_____ _____

_____ _____

_____ _____

_____ _____

_____ _____

_____ _____

_____ _____

_____ _____

_____ _____

_____ _____

_____ _____

Chapter 1 Supplemental Forms

Form 1.1 Student information

Teacher: _____

School: _____

School year: _____

Program: _____

Student Name Student FTE or ID Number	Student Disability	Current Psychological Date	Current Eligibility Date	IEP Start/End Dates	Hours Served in Special Education	Hours Served in Regular Education	Medical Concerns and/or Medications	Additional Information

Shelton, C. F., and Pollingue, A. B. *The Exceptional Teacher's Handbook: The First-Year Special Education Teacher's Guide for Success.* ©2000. Corwin Press, Inc.

Form 1.2 Classroom modifications

Student Name: _____   Date: _____

Grade: _____ Subject: _____   Period: _____

Regular education teacher: _____

Special education teacher: _____

Note: —The classroom modifications checked below must be implemented in order for the student to experi-ence success in his or her inclusive class or classes. The modifications selected are in compliance with the student's individualized educational program. In addition, the modifications are appropriate based on the student's identified and documented learning deficits.

_____ Preferential seating

_____ Modified test (circle):

    - Oral test

    - Open book test

    - Shortened test

    - Eliminate choices on multiple choice test

    - Extended time to complete test

    - Test may be read to student

_____ Student may leave class for resource assistance (this must be arranged in advance).

_____ Modified assignments (circle):

    - Shortened assignments (fewer math problems, fewer pages to read, and so on).

    - Extended time for assignment completion.

    - Allow student to utilize several alternatives to obtain information for reports: tapes, interviews, reading, experience, or making something, and so on.

_____ Assignment book

_____ Mark student's correct and acceptable work only.

_____ Praise or reward student for appropriate behavior.

_____ Note-taking assistance

_____ Recognize and give credit for student's oral participation in class.

_____ Utilize cross-age tutoring.

_____ Avoid placing student under pressure of time or competition.

_____ Written assignments may be typed.

_____ Student may utilize cursive or manuscript writing.

_____ Give directions verbally and in written form.

_____ Utilize a behavior point system.

_____ Quietly repeat directions to student.

_____ Taped text/lectures.

_____ Special equipment needed or other recommended modifications (list):

_____

_____

_____

_____

Shelton, C. F., and Pollingue, A. B. *The Exceptional Teacher's Handbook: The First-Year Special Education Teacher's Guide for Success.* ©2000. Corwin Press, Inc.

Form 1.3 Correspondence log

Teacher: _____   Month/Year: _____

Date: _____
Method: Telephone   Letter   Fax   School note   E-mail
Corresponded with: Mr.   Ms.   Mrs. _____
In reference to:

_____

_____

_____

_____

Date: _____
Method: Telephone   Letter   Fax   School note   E-mail
Corresponded with: Mr.   Ms.   Mrs. _____
In reference to:

_____

_____

_____

_____

Date: _____
Method: Telephone   Letter   Fax   School note   E-mail
Corresponded with: Mr.   Ms.   Mrs. _____
In reference to:

_____

_____

_____

_____

Date: _____
Method: Telephone   Letter   Fax   School note   E-mail
Corresponded with: Mr.   Ms.   Mrs. _____
In reference to:

_____

_____

_____

_____

Form 1.4   Paraprofessional's classroom responsibilities checklist

Teacher's Name: _____   School Year: _____

Paraprofessional's Name: _____   Program: _____

_____ Record daily student attendance   Additional tasks (list):

_____ File students' papers   _____

_____ Grade students' academic work   _____

_____ Assist the teacher with assigned
        school duties   _____

_____ Monitor students during recess   _____

_____ Tutor students in deficit academic
        areas   _____

_____ Assist students in computer lab   _____

_____ Assist students in the cafeteria   _____

_____ Assist students in media center   _____

_____ Monitor/assist students arriving
        on school bus or special van   _____

_____ Assist teacher with classroom
        administrative duties   _____

_____ Assist students in bathroom   _____

_____ Assist students in the cafeteria   _____

_____ Maintain behavior point sheets   _____

_____ Laminate instructional materials   _____

_____ Make copies of instructional
        materials   _____

_____ Organize classroom materials   _____

_____ Assist with academic groups   _____

Form 1.5 Present levels of performance

Teacher: _____

School: _____

School Year: _____

Program: _____

Student Name	Word Recognition Level	Reading Comprehension Level	Written Expression Level	Spelling Level	Math Calculation Level	Math Reasoning Level	Adaptive Behavior Level

Shelton, C. F., and Pollingue, A. B. *The Exceptional Teacher's Handbook: The First-Year Special Education Teacher's Guide for Success.*
©2000. Corwin Press, Inc.

Form 1.6 Student emergency information

Student name: _____

Date of birth: _____

Age: _____   Present grade: _____

Student FTE or identification number: _____

Parent name: _____

Address: _____

Mailing address: _____

Home telephone number: _____

Mother work number: _____

    E-Mail address: _____

    Cellular telephone number: _____

Father work number: _____

    E-Mail address: _____

    Cellular telephone number: _____

Emergency contact person: _____

Emergency telephone: _____

Significant medical problems: _____

_____

_____

_____

Medications: _____

Allergies: _____

Wears glasses or contact lenses: Yes or No

Transportation to school: Bus   Car   Daycare van   Walk

Transportation from school: Bus   Car   Daycare van   Walk

Shelton, C. F., and Pollingue, A. B. *The Exceptional Teacher's Handbook: The First-Year Special Education Teacher's Guide for Success.* ©2000. Corwin Press, Inc.

Form 1.7A   Classroom supply checklist (non-instructional)

Teacher: _____   School Year: _____

Class: _____   Room number: _____

_____ White copy paper (8 1/2 X 11)

_____ Color copy paper (8 1/2 X 11)

    _____ Green   _____ Gray

    _____ Ivory   _____ Pink

    _____ Goldenrod   _____ Lavender

    _____ Salmon   _____ Tan

    _____ Canary   _____ Blue

_____ NCR paper (8 1/2 X 11) Wht/Yellow 2-part

_____ NCR paper (8 1/2 X 11) Wht/Yellow/Pink 3-part

_____ Computer paper (Laser or other)

_____ Notebook paper

    _____ Three-ring 10 1/4 X 8, ruled

    (College or wide rule)

    _____ Wire bound, 11 X 8 1/2

    _____ Composition book 10 X 8

_____ Primary practice paper

_____ Construction paper

    _____ 9 X 12 assorted

    _____ 12 X 18 assorted

    _____ 18 X 24 assorted

_____ Art craft paper

_____ Bulletin board paper

_____ Bulletin board border

_____ Teacher plan book

_____ Teacher grade book

_____ Sentence strips

    (3 inch X 24 inch)

_____ Chart tablets

_____ Chart stand

_____ Legal Pads 8 1/2 X 11

    _____ Canary

    _____ White

_____ Index cards 8 1/2 X 11

_____ Adhesive note pads

    _____ 2 X 3

    _____ 3 X 3

    _____ 3 X 5

    _____ Color: _____

_____ Manila file folders

_____ File guides A-Z letter

_____ Transparency film

    _____ Acetate writing roll

    _____ Single sheet

_____ Report covers

    _____ 3 fasteners

    _____ Double pockets

    _____ 3 fasteners double pockets

Form 1.7B Classroom supply checklist (non-instructional)

_____ Ballpoint pens

_____ Black ink

_____ Blue ink

_____ Red ink

_____ Pencils

_____ #2 standard

_____ Red correcting

_____ Primary

_____ Mechanical

_____ Permanent markers

_____ Black

_____ Blue

_____ Green

_____ Red

_____ Highlighter markers

_____ Set of six highlighters

_____ Yellow

_____ Orange

_____ Blue

_____ Transparency markers

_____ Black

_____ Blue

_____ Red

_____ Green

_____ Notebook binders

_____ Three-ring, 1 inch diameter

_____ Three-ring, 1 1/2 inch diameter

_____ Three-ring, 2 inch diameter

_____ Rubber bands

_____ Stapler

_____ Staples

_____ Gem clips

_____ Small

_____ Large

_____ Ideal clamps

_____ Felt stamp pads

_____ Black

_____ Red

_____ Blue

_____ Green

_____ Glue

_____ White squeeze

_____ Glue stick

_____ Rubber cement

_____ Paste, jar

_____ Chalk

_____ White

_____ Colored

_____ Yellow

_____ Chalk holder

_____ Crayons

_____ Colored pencils

_____ Colored markers

_____ Rulers

_____ Meter sticks

_____ Folder labels

_____ Thumb tacks

_____ Scissors and shears

_____ Teacher shears

_____ Student scissors

Shelton, C. F., and Pollingue, A. B. *The Exceptional Teacher's Handbook: The First-Year Special Education Teacher's Guide for Success.* ©2000. Corwin Press, Inc.

Form 1.7C   Classroom supply checklist (non-instructional)

_____ Masking tape

_____ Adhesive tape

_____ Tape dispenser

_____ Paper punchers

_____ 3-hole punch

_____ 2-hole punch

_____ 1-hole punch

_____ Computer supplies

_____ Computer diskettes (3.5 inch)

_____ Mouse pad

_____ Diskette storage box

_____ Computer screen and CD cleaner

_____ Printer cartridge (black or color)

_____ Science fair project boards

_____ Surge protector, six outlets

_____ Anti-bacterial soap

_____ Paper towels

_____ Facial tissues

_____ Window cleaner or other cleaning solution

_____ Typewriter correction fluid

_____ White

_____ Yellow

_____ Other

_____ Disposable latex gloves

Additional list of items to order:

_____   _____

_____   _____

_____   _____

_____   _____

_____   _____

_____   _____

_____   _____

_____   _____

_____   _____

Form 1.8   Classroom inventory checklist

Teacher: _____   School Year: _____

Class: _____   Room Number: _____

Item	Quantity	Item Description and Serial Number	Condition of Item

Shelton, C. F., and Pollingue, A. B. *The Exceptional Teacher's Handbook: The First-Year Special Education Teacher's Guide for Success.* ©2000. Corwin Press, Inc.

Form 1.9   Exceptional student monitor information

Student: _____   Date: _____

Subject: _____   Teacher: _____

Note: The information recorded on this monitor form will be shared with the student
and his or her parents when appropriate and filed for documentation.

Class participation: Pass: _____   Fail: _____

Class/daily work: Pass: _____   Fail: _____

Homework: Pass: _____   Fail: _____

Quiz grades: Pass: _____   Fail: _____

Test grades: Pass: _____   Fail: _____

On-task behavior: Good: _____   Fair: _____   Poor: _____

Tardy/absent: T: _____   Ab: _____

Overall performance: Pass: _____   Fail: _____

Teacher request conference: Yes: _____   No: _____

Teacher concerns:

_____

_____

_____

_____

_____

Return form to: _____

Due date: _____

Shelton, C. F., and Pollingue, A. B. *The Exceptional Teacher's Handbook: The First-Year Special Education Teacher's Guide for Success.* ©2000. Corwin Press, Inc.

Form 1.10 Exceptional student monitor results summary

Student Name: _____   Report Date: _____

Report Period: _____

Note: — This form is to be utilized as a summary for the *Exceptional Student Monitor Information* form (Form 1-9). Review each student's completed monitor forms and place check marks in problem areas. The summary form is a quick reference of student progress in inclusive settings.

Subject	Class Participation	Class Daily Work	Homework Grades	Quiz Grades	Test Grades	On Task Behavior	Overall Performance	Tardy	Absent

Teacher Concerns:

_____

_____

_____

_____

_____

_____

Form 1.11   Behavior contract

Student's name: _____   Date: _____

Teacher's name: _____   Grade: _____

Contract starts: _____   Class: _____

Contract ends: _____

Contract review dates: _____   _____   _____   _____   _____

Contract Terms

The student will

_____

_____

_____

_____

The teacher will

_____

_____

_____

_____

The student must fulfill his or her part of the contract in order to receive the agreed-

upon reward from the teacher.

Student's signature: _____

Teacher's signature: _____

Shelton, C. F., and Pollingue, A. B. *The Exceptional Teacher's Handbook: The First-Year Special Education Teacher's Guide for Success.* ©2000. Corwin Press, Inc.

Understanding Students with Disabilities

The first-year special education teacher should allocate a tremendous amount of time prior to the start of the new school year to reviewing and analyzing all information related to the students on his or her caseload. The authors recommend that the new teacher have a clear understanding of each student's needs from an educational, physiological, and emotional perspective before attempting to plan and implement instructional programs. Students with disabilities bring a spectrum of expectations to the school experience. Each student possesses unique learning characteristics that will possibly challenge the instructor and can potentially cause the school experience to be one of devastation for the student. The goals of the new special education teacher should be to provide a quality educational program based on student need, promote student success inside and outside the special education classroom, and build a positive rapport between home and school. The accomplishment of these goals will most likely result in a positive school experience for the student and the first-year special education teacher.

In Chapter 2, the authors present a procedure that is designed to assist the new teacher in his or her quest to understand the special student. The procedure is divided into three major sections. Section 1 guides the teacher through the process of conducting a thorough survey of each student's current IEP and other pertinent student information. A checklist and student profile form is provided to assist in this review. Section 2 provides a selection of student inventories and surveys to help the new teacher obtain a deeper understanding of his or her assigned students. Finally, in Section 3, the authors provide a review of all disabilities recognized in the federal regulations of the *Individuals with Disabilities Act 1997*. The review includes the legal definitions for all recognized disabilities and additional general information for disabilities that the new teacher will most likely encounter. The final section of this chapter is intended to serve as a quick reference for the reader and is extremely helpful for the interrelated or cross-categorical teacher.

Section 1: Reviewing Student Information

The reviewing and analyzing of student information is tedious and time-consuming. However, this process is typically the initial step prior to designing and implementing a successful educational program for all students. Critical information related to each student is usually contained in a confidential file folder that is secured and maintained in the special education teacher's classroom. However, general student information such as attendance and transcripts can be obtained from the student's permanent school record. This record is traditionally maintained in the main office area of the school building. All information should be current and reviewed thoroughly by the new special education teacher. The authors have created the **Student Folder Checklist** (Form 2.1) and **Student Profile** (Form 2.2) that will assist the new teacher with the review process and the recording of all pertinent student information. The special education teacher should have possession or access to the following documents for every student on his or her caseload:

Individualized education program plan

Eligibility document

Classroom performance (regular and special class)

Classroom observations

School discipline information

School attendance information

Student transition plan

Vision and hearing screening results

Student transportation information

Student medical information

Form 2.1 Student folder checklist

Directions: Complete a *Student Folder Checklist* form for each IEP Folder in your possession. The teacher should read each IEP thoroughly and annotate all questions or concerns in the comments section of the form.

Student Name: _____ Date: _____

Student Disability: _____ Grade: _____

Information	Yes	No	Comments
Individualized Education Plan (Current I.E.P.)			
Eligibility Document			
Classroom Performance			
Classroom Observation			
School Discipline Information			
School Attendance Information			
Student Transition Plan			
Vision and Hearing Screening Results			
Transportation Information			
Medical Information			
Miscellaneous Information (List):			

Shelton, C. F., and Pollingue, A. B. *The Exceptional Teacher's Handbook: The First-Year Special Education Teacher's Guide for Success.* ©2000. Corwin Press, Inc.

Form 2.2   Student profile

School year: _____

Student name: _____   Date:_____

Disability: _____   Age: _____   Grade: _____

Directions: Complete a *Student Profile* form for each student on your caseload. The form
should be completed as the student's IEP information is reviewed.

Student's academic
strengths:

_____

_____

_____

_____

Student's academic
weaknesses:

_____

_____

_____

_____

Student's behavior or emotional
issues:

_____

_____

_____

_____

Student's adaptive behavior
issues:

_____

_____

_____

_____

Additional information:

_____

_____

_____

_____

Section 2: Student Surveys and Inventories

The first-year special education teacher can utilize a multitude of strategies to obtain a more comprehensive perspective of each exceptional student on his or her caseload. The authors recommend student surveys and inventories as a means of obtaining information and gaining insight into how each student processes information in the academic environment and his or her preferred learning style. These instruments are subjective by design and usually provide the student with the opportunity to communicate thoughts, feelings, and opinions regarding his or her educational needs to the special education teacher. In this section, the authors provide the new teacher with simple surveys and inventories designed to extract essential student information. The surveys and inventories make for good independent student activities during the first days of school. The student inventories and surveys found in this section are

- **Student Academic Inventory** (Form 2.3A-B): The inventory is completed by the special education teacher after he or she has reviewed all the student information referred to in the first section of this chapter. The instructor can utilize this form when developing classroom modifications for students in inclusive settings.

- **Learning Style Survey** (Forms 2–4A-B): The survey is to be completed by the student on an independent basis. However, students who do not read may have assistance with completing the form from a teacher or peer. The results of the survey will provide the teacher with information regarding the student's preferred learning style.

- **Student Interest Inventory** (Form 2.5): The survey is to be completed by the student on an independent basis. However, students who do not read may have assistance with completing the form from a teacher or peer. The results of the survey will provide the teacher with a greater understanding of the student's personal and school interest.

- **Career Survey** (Form 2.6A-D): The purpose of the **Career Survey** is to promote the importance of career planning and exploration for elementary (4th and 5th grades), middle, and high school students. The survey can be incorporated into the transition plans of students with disabilities when appropriate. The student can complete the survey with the special education teacher's assistance if the student does not read.

Form 2.3A Student academic inventory

Student Name: _____   Date: _____

Current Grade: _____   Age: _____   Disability: _____

Directions: Complete the inventory below upon reviewing the student's current IEP assessments (formal and informal) and classroom performance information.

Sources from which the student can receive, process, and retrieve academic information	Strength	Weakness	Delivery method for academic instruction	Strength	Weakness
Textbook			Direct		
Worksheets			Independent Study		
Lecture			Peer Tutor		
Class Discussions			One-to-one Teacher Assistance		
Audio-Visual Material			Small Group		
Hands-on Experiences			Large Group		
Observation			Computer-Managed		
Other: (list)			Other: (list)		

Shelton, C. F., and Pollingue, A. B. *The Exceptional Teacher's Handbook: The First-Year Special Education Teacher's Guide for Success.* ©2000. Corwin Press, Inc.

Form 2.3B Student academic inventory

Academic testing formats that measure degree of skill mastery	Strength	Weakness	Academic course assignments	Strength	Weakness
Written Test			Short Papers		
Oral Test			Worksheets		
Short Answer Test			Oral Reports		
Essay Test			Textbook Exercises		
Multiple Choice Test			Course Projects		
True-False Test			Presentations		
Matching Test			Vocabulary Exercises		
Computation Test			Science Labs		
Other: (List)			Other: (List)		

Shelton, C. F., and Pollingue, A. B. The Exceptional Teacher's Handbook: The First-Year Special Education Teacher's Guide for Success. ©2000. Corwin Press, Inc.

Form 2.4A   Student learning styles survey

Part A

Student Name: _____   Date: _____

Grade: _____   Class: _____

Directions: The *Student Learning Styles Survey* is design to assist teachers in planning
and implementing effective instructional programs. Please answer the
questions below to the best of your ability in order to assist the teacher in
obtaining a true understanding of your learning style.

1. Rate the type of test you prefer on a scale of 1 to 5 (1 is most preferred).
   _____ True/False   _____ Fill-in-the-blank
   _____ Multiple Choice   _____ Discussion
   _____ Matching   _____ Other (list): _____

2. Check the situation when note-taking is most difficult.
   _____ During class lectures   _____ From chalkboard
   _____ From the overhead projector   _____ Other (list): _____

3. Check the situation where you learn the best.
   _____ Reading material by myself   _____ Class lecture
   _____ Working with a peer   _____ Listening to material on tape
   _____ Other (list/explain): _____

4. Check the environments where you like to study.
   _____ In my bedroom   _____ A quiet place
   _____ A place with music   _____ In the library
   _____ Other (list/explain): _____

5. When do you study best?
   _____ Morning   _____ Afternoon   _____ Night

6. Check the school subject in which you have the most difficulty.
   _____ Reading   _____ English   _____ Writing
   _____ Math   _____ Science   _____ Social Studies
   _____ Other (list):_____

Shelton, C. F., and Pollingue, A. B. *The Exceptional Teacher's Handbook: The First-Year Special Education Teacher's Guide for Success.* ©2000. Corwin Press, Inc.

Form 2.4B   Student learning styles survey

Directions: Please place a check mark in the column beside each statement that applies to you. The comments section may be used to provide further details to help the teacher better understand your needs.

CHECK   COMMENTS

	I can read test given in class to myself.	
	I can take notes in class without assistance.	
	I can read class textbooks out loud or to myself.	
	I understand the content in my class textbooks.	
	I can communicate with my teachers.	
	Class material is easier for me to understand when we do labs or other hands-on activities.	
	I maintain an assignment book on a daily basis.	
	I am organized for each class on a daily basis.	
	I have a set study time or schedule and location.	
	I prepare for tests and quizzes in advance.	

Student Comments: _____

_____

Shelton, C. F., and Pollingue, A. B. *The Exceptional Teacher's Handbook: The First-Year Special Education Teacher's Guide for Success.* ©2000. Corwin Press, Inc.

Form 2.5   Student interest survey

Student Name:_____   Date: _____

Directions: Please answer all the questions listed below. The *Student Interest Survey* will
            help your teacher get to know you a little better. A teacher, parent, or friend
            can read the survey to you and assist with recording your responses to the
            survey questions.

1. I like to read about _____.

2. In my free time I like to _____.

3. I like people who _____.

4. My favorite author is _____.

5. When I grow up I want to be _____.

6. My favorite subject in school is _____.

7. My hobby/hobbies are _____.

8. I don't like books that _____.

9. The place I would like to visit most is _____.

10. My favorite vacation was _____.

11. The thing I like to do most is _____.

12. What I want most in the world is _____.

13. I wish _____.

14. My favorite song is _____.

15. My favorite book is _____.

16. My favorite color is _____.

17. My favorite food is _____.

18. My favorite movie is _____.

19. My favorite sport is _____.

20. This school year I will _____

Form 2.6A Career survey: fourth and fifth grade students

Student Name: _____ Date: _____

Directions: Students need to begin the task of career exploration and planning as early as possible. The *Career Interest Survey* is a good start to the process. Please do your best and complete the entire survey.

1. List as many jobs as you can:

_____

_____

2. Why is it important to prepare for a job?

_____

_____

3. What have you studied in school that might be useful for a particular job?

_____

_____

4. List three jobs that are of interest to you:

_____

_____

5. What jobs are available in your community?

_____

_____

6. Describe the jobs of your family members:

_____

_____

7. Do you think it is important for people who work together to get along? (Yes or No)
Explain:

_____

_____

Shelton, C. F., and Pollingue, A. B. *The Exceptional Teacher's Handbook: The First-Year Special Education Teacher's Guide for Success.* ©2000. Corwin Press, Inc.

Form 2.6B   Career survey: middle and high school students

---

8. List some ways in which a person could become known as a "good worker:"

_____

_____

9. Would you prefer to work alone or with others?

_____

10. Would you prefer to work outside or inside?

_____

11. Would you prefer to work where it is quiet or where it is noisy?

_____

Please use the lines below to tell me about your "dream job or career:"

_____

_____

_____

_____

_____

_____

_____

_____

_____

_____

_____

_____

_____

_____

_____

_____

_____

_____

Form 2.6C   Career survey: middle and high school students

Student Name: _____   Date: _____

Directions: Students need to begin the task of career exploration and planning as early as possible. The *Career Interest Survey* is a good start to the process. Please do your best and complete the entire survey.

1. What are some of your career interests at the present time?

    _____

    _____

2. List the school courses that you have taken or are presently enrolled in that would be useful in the careers of interest to you:

    _____

    _____

3. What are the educational requirements of the careers that you are considering?

    _____

    _____

4. What actions have you taken to investigate your career interest?

    _____

    _____

5. Where can you find career information?

    _____

    _____

6. What are the characteristics of a "good employee?"

    _____

    _____

7. Do you think it is important for people who work together to get along? (Yes or No) Explain:

    _____

    _____

8. Do you think it is important for people to balance work and leisure activities? Explain:

    _____

    _____

9. What are your career goals?

    _____

    _____

Shelton, C. F., and Pollingue, A. B. *The Exceptional Teacher's Handbook: The First-Year Special Education Teacher's Guide for Success.* ©2000. Corwin Press, Inc.

Form 2.6D   Career survey: middle and high school students

Please use the lines below to write a career plan:

_____

_____

_____

_____

_____

_____

_____

_____

_____

_____

_____

_____

_____

_____

_____

_____

_____

_____

_____

_____

_____

_____

_____

_____

_____

_____

_____

_____

Section 3: Review of Recognized Disabilities

Special education is constantly evolving and changing in both philosophies and practices as a result of the tremendous amount of research conducted in the field every year. Therefore, it is imperative that teachers be current in the field and their respective areas of expertise. One of the most prominent changes in practices is the utilization of the cross-categorical or interrelated classrooms. These classrooms are designed to serve students with different disabilities but similar levels of severity for academic instruction or support. As a result of this trend, the authors recommend that new special education teachers review current information on all recognized disabilities prior to the start of school and continue throughout the entire year in order to meet the needs of a diverse group of students with disabilities. In the following pages, the authors provide the reader with the legal definitions for all disabilities that are currently recognized in the new regulations of the *Individuals with Disabilities Act 1997*. In addition, supplemental information is provided for the disabilities that the new special education teacher will most likely encounter. All information is presented in an abbreviated format and intended only as a quick review or reference and not an in-depth study. The authors recommend up dating the information provided on a yearly basis.

Autism

Legally Defined Autism means a developmental disability significantly affecting verbal and nonverbal communication and social interaction, generally evident before age 3, that adversely affects a child's educational performance. Other characteristics often associated with autism are engagement in repetitive activities and stereotyped movements, resistance to environmental change or change in daily routines, and unusual responses to sensory experiences. The term does not apply if a child's educational performance is adversely affected primarily because the child has an emotional disturbance, as defined in paragraph (b)(4) of this section *(Federal Register/No. 48*, Volume 64/Section 300.7 (c)(1) (i)/1999).

Typical Eligibility Information Required

Psychological evaluation

Educational evaluation

Communication evaluation

Behavioral observations

Developmental history

Deaf-Blindness

Legally Defined Deaf-blindness means concomitant hearing and visual impairments, the combination of which causes such severe communication and other developmental and educational needs that they cannot be accommodated in special education programs solely for children with deafness or children with blindness (*Federal Register/No. 48*, Volume 64/Section 300.7 (c) (2)/1999).

Typical Eligibility Information Required

Audiological evaluation

Otological evaluation

Ophthalmological evaluation

Deafness

Legally Defined Deafness means a hearing impairment that is so severe that the child is impaired in processing linguistic information through hearing, with or without amplification, that adversely affects a child's educational performance *(Federal Register/No. 48*, Volume 64/Section 300.7 (c) (3)/1999).

Typical Eligibility Information Required

Otological evaluation

Audiological evaluation

Emotional Disturbance

Legally Defined

(i)   The term means a condition exhibiting one or more of the following characteristics over a long period of time and to a marked degree that adversely affects a child's educational performance:

(a)   An inability to learn that cannot be explained by intellectual, sensory, or health factors.

(b)   An inability to build or maintain satisfactory interpersonal relationships with peers and teachers.

(c)   Inappropriate types of behavior or feelings under normal circumstances.

(d)   A general pervasive mood of unhappiness or depression.

(e)   A tendency to develop physical symptoms or fears associated with personal or school problems.

(ii) The term includes schizophrenia. The term does not apply to children who are socially maladjusted, unless it is determined that they have an emotional disturbance *(Federal Register/No. 48,* Volume 64/ Section 300.7 (c) (4) (i) (ii) /1999).

Behavioral Disorders

Behavioral disorders and emotional disturbance are generally categorized by whether they are primarily *externalizing* or *internalizing.* Externalizing behaviors are generally aggressive behaviors expressed outwardly toward other persons. Internalizing behaviors are those expressed in a more socially withdrawn fashion. The following are examples of behavioral characteristics for each category (Smith and Luckasson, 1992, p. 307):

Externalizing Behaviors	*Internalizing Behaviors*
Hitting other children	Depression
Cursing at a teacher	Withdrawal
Hyperactivity	Fears and phobias
Stealing	Anorexia and bulimia
Arson	Elective mutism

Typical Eligibility Information Required

Psychological evaluation

Educational evaluation

Behavioral observations

Social history

Hearing Impairment

Legally Defined   Hearing impairment means an impairment in hearing, whether permanent or fluctuating, that adversely affects a child's educational performance but that is not included under the definition of deafness in this section *(Federal Register/No. 48,* Volume 64/Section 300.7 (c) (5)/1999).

Types of Hearing Loss

1) Conductive hearing losses indicate that the damage or disease is located in the outer or middle ear. These losses may be due to such conditions as fluid in the normally air-filled middle ear, an abnormally small ear canal, too much ear wax, or malfunctioning or malformed ossicles.

2) Sensorineural hearing losses result from an abnormality or disease in the inner ear, the cochlea, or the auditory nerve. Such conditions as a sudden blockages of circulation in or an infection of the inner ear, a leak in the inner ear fluid, a buildup of fluid in the inner ear, or tumors on

the auditory nerve may be treated surgically or medically; hearing loss may be prevented or hearing improved if treatment is initiated before permanent damage occurs.

3) Congenital hearing losses occur during fetal development or during birth. Most congenital hearing losses are sensorineural and due to either genetic defects or nongenetic factors such as rubella, diabetes, or an underactive thyroid in the mother during pregnancy (Gearheart, 1993, pp. 234–235).

Assistive Listening Devices for Hearing Impaired Students

Hearing aids

Auditory trainers

Audio loop

Typical Eligibility Information Required

Audiological evaluation

Otological evaluation

Educational evaluation

Table 2.1   Levels of hearing impairment

Hearing Thresholds	Ability to Understand Speech
26-40 dB	Difficulty only with faint speech
41-70 dB	Frequent difficulty with normal speech
71-90 dB	Can understand only shouted or amplified speech
91 dB or more	Usually can't hear any speech

(Schildroth and Karchmer, 1986, p. 12)

Mental Retardation

Legally Defined   Mental retardation means significantly sub-average general intellectual functioning, existing concurrently with deficits in adaptive behavior and manifested during the developmental period, which adversely affect a child's educational performance *(Federal Register/No. 48*, Volume 64/Section 300.7 (c) (6)/1999).

Etiology   On the basis of current knowledge, approximately 25 percent of all cases of mental retardation are known to be caused by biological abnormalities. Chromosomal and metabolic disorders—such as Down's syndrome, fragile X syndrome, and phenylketonuria (PKU)—are the most common disorders manifesting mental retardation. Mental retardation associated with these disorders is usually diagnosed at birth or relatively early in childhood, and the severity is generally moderate to profound.

No specific biological causes can be identified in the remaining 75 percent of the cases. The level of intellectual impairment of a person with no known cause is usually mild, with an I.Q. between 50 to 70. The diagnosis of mild retardation is not usually made before grade school. In mild mental retardation, a familial pattern is often seen in parents and siblings (Kapland and Sadock, 1991, p. 686).

Prenatal Factors

Rubella (German Measles)

Cytomegalic inclusion diseases

Syphilis

AIDS

Complications of pregnancy

Substance abuse

Chromosomal Abnormalities

Down's syndrome

Cat-cry (cri-du-chat) syndrome

Fragile X syndrome

Rett's syndrome

Genetic Factors

Phenylketonuria (PKU)

Menkes' disease

Hartnup disease

Galactosemia

Glycogen storage disease

Acquired Childhood Diseases

Infection: encephalitis and meningitis

Head trauma

Other issues include cardiac arrest, asphyxia, chronic exposure to lead, and chemotherapy

Intellectual Functioning   Mental retardation is classified according to the degree of intellectual impairment. The AAMD identifies four levels of mental retardation and the IQ range for each (Grossman, 1983):

Retardation Level	*Suggested IQ Range*
Mild	50–55 to approximately 70
Moderate	35–40 to 50–55
Severe	20–25 to 35–40
Profound	Below 20 or 25

Typical Eligibility Information Required

Psychological evaluation

Educational evaluation

Adaptive behavior evaluation

Relevant medical information

Multiple Disability

Legally Defined   Multiple disability means concomitant impairments (such as mental retardation-blindness, mental retardation-orthopedic impairment, etc.), the combination of which causes such severe educational needs that they cannot be accommodated in the special education programs solely for one of the impairments. The term does not include deaf-blindness *(Federal Register/No. 48,* Volume 64/Section 300.7 (c) (7)/1999).

Orthopedic Impairment

Legally Defined   Orthopedic impairment means a severe orthopedic impairment that adversely affects a child's educational performance. The term includes impairment caused by congenital anomaly (for example, clubfoot, absence of some member, etc.), impairments caused by disease (e.g., poliomyelitis, bone tuberculosis, etc.), and impairments from other causes (e.g., cerebral palsy, amputations, and fractures or burns that cause contractures) *(Federal Register/No. 48*, Volume 64/Section 300.7 (c) (8)/1999.

Typical Eligibility Information Required

Medical examination

Educational evaluation

Psychological evaluation

Other Health Impaired

Legally Defined Other health impaired means having limited strength, vitality or alertness, including a heightened alertness to environmental stimuli, that results in limited alertness with respect to the educational environment, that (i) is due to chronic or acute health problems such as asthma, attention deficit disorder or attention deficit hyperactivity disorder, diabetes, epilepsy, a heart condition, hemophilia, lead poisoning, leukemia, nephritis, rheumatic fever, and sickle cell anemia; and (ii) adversely affects a child's educational performance *(Federal Register/No. 48*, Volume 64/Section 300.7 (c) (9)/1999).

Typical Eligibility Information Required

Medical examination

Educational evaluation

Psychological evaluation

Specific Learning Disability

Legally Defined

(i) Specific learning disability term means a disorder in one or more of the basic psychological processes involved in understanding or in using language, spoken or written, that may manifest itself in an imperfect ability to listen, think, speak, read, write, spell, or to do mathematical calculations, including such conditions as perceptual disabilities, brain injury, minimal brain dysfunction, dyslexia, and developmental aphasia.

(ii) Disorders not included: The term does not include learning problems that are primarily the result of visual, hearing, or motor disabilities, of mental retardation, of emotional disturbance, or of environmental, cultural, or economic disadvantage *(Federal Register/No. 48*, Volume 64/Section 300.7 (c) (10)(i and ii)/1999).

General Information The authors can find no nationally consistent method for determining whether a student has a specific learning disability. The utilization of discrepancy scores and formulas is one of the most common approaches for identifying students with specific learning disabilities. In this approach, a standardized intelligence test and standardized achievement test is administered to the student. The results from the intelligence test reveal the student's potential, whereas the achievement test results demonstrate the student's actual academic performance. The student's standard scores on both test are reviewed and evaluated for significant discrepancies.

The following is a list of characteristics of the SLD student:

- Mixed dominance
- Learning disability in family
- Directional confusion
- Sequencing problems
- No concept of time
- Retrieval difficulty
- Attention problems
- Poor motor control
- Disorganization
- Reversals
- Poor oral reading
- Inability to copy
- Poor spelling
- Trouble with written expression
- Leaky memory
- Problem with attitude, motivation, and creative behavior

Typical Eligibility Information Required

Psychological evaluation

Comprehensive educational evaluation

Classroom observation

Analyzed samples of work

Relevant medical information

Speech or Language Impairment

Legally Defined   Speech or language impairment means a communication disorder, such as stuttering, impaired articulation, language impairment, or a voice impairment, that adversely affects a child's educational performance *(Federal Register/No. 48*, Volume 64/Section 300.7 (c) (11)/1999).

General Information

Speech disorders: voice, articulation, and fluency

Language disorders: form (phonology, morphology, and syntax), content (semantics), and use (pragmatics).

Typical Eligibility Information Required

Oral peripheral examination

Articulation evaluation

Language evaluation

Voice evaluation

Fluency

Traumatic Brain Injury

Legally Defined   Traumatic brain injury means an acquired injury to the brain caused by an external physical force, resulting in total or partial functional disability or psychosocial impairment, or both, that adversely affects a child's educational performance. The term applies to open or closed head injuries resulting in impairments in one or more areas, such as cognition; language; memory; attention; reasoning; abstract thinking; judgment; problem-solving; sensory, perceptual and motor abilities; psychosocial behavior; physical functions; information processing and speech. The term does not apply to brain injuries that are congenital or degenerative, or to brain injuries induced by birth trauma *(Federal Register/No. 48,* Volume 64/Section 300.7 (c) 12)/1999).

Typical Eligibility Information Required

A formal report of pre-injury functioning

Medical report

Psychological evaluation

Visual Impairment

Legally Defined   Visual impairment including blindness means an impairment in vision that, even with correction, adversely affects a child's educational performance. The term includes both partial sight and blindness *(Federal Register/No. 48,* Volume 64/Section 300.7 (c) (13)/1999).

Typical Eligibility Information Required

Ophthalmologic evaluation

Educational evaluation

Placing Students in Inclusive Settings

Inclusion is the placing of students with disabilities in an educational environment with nondisabled students for a designated period of time during the regular school day. The placement can be of an academic, nonacademic, or extracurricular nature. The actual placing of students with disabilities in inclusive settings begins with the IEP team. The new regulations of IDEA '97 dictate that the IEP team explore every opportunity for placing students with exceptionalities in appropriate inclusive settings to the maximum extent possible. The team must write a statement explaining and substantiating all placement decisions. After the decision is made to place the student in an inclusive setting, the special education teacher must accomplish a multitude of the tasks that accompany this action. The key to successful inclusive placements of students with disabilities is collaboration, communication, and prior planning.

In the pages that follow, the authors provide checklists, surveys, supplemental forms, and helpful hints that will assist and support the new teacher through the entire inclusion process. The chapter is divided into four sections. Each section targets some aspect of the inclusion process. In Section 1, the authors suggest various issues for the IEP team to explore before making their final decision to place a student in an inclusive setting. The authors have found that students usually have positive inclusive experiences if the IEP team members have reviewed all available information and discussed significant student issues before making their final placement recommendation.

In Section 2, the authors provide the new teacher with a selection of classroom modifications, suggestions for modifying tests, a materials list for the inclusive student, and teacher tips for special and regular education teachers. The IEP team should select modifications and strategies that are realistic and appropriate for the students handicapping condition. All selected modifications should be included in the classroom modification section of the student's individualized education plan.

Section 3 assists the new special education teacher as he or she begins the tedious process of selecting teachers for the student being placed in an inclusive setting. Although the IEP team makes the decision to place a student in an inclusive setting, the special education teacher is typically responsible for selecting the student's regular education teacher or teachers. The keys to successful placement are finding teachers that are receptive to the inclusion approach and that have instructional styles that are conducive to the student's learning style. When an appropriate match is found, a copy of classroom modifications stated in the student's IEP must be given to the regular education teacher or teachers.

In Section 4, the authors provide the materials necessary for the first-year special education teacher to monitor students' progress in the regular education setting. Students should be monitored on a regular basis in order to address issues or concerns as they occur. The new teacher will find monitor forms and summary sheets to assist with the tracking of student progress in inclusive settings.

Step 1: The Inclusion Decision

The IEP team must thoroughly review and discuss all current information relating to the student before making their final placement decision. The special education teacher should gather and prepare in advance the following student information for review by the team:

- Student's school attendance information
- Student's discipline information
- Student's current levels of academic performance
- Student's current status of medical condition (if applicable)
- Classroom observation information
- Regular education teacher summary report or reports

The following forms are presented in this section:

Form 3.1   The inclusive decision

Student Name: _____   Date: _____

Grade: _____   Age: _____   Disability: _____

Team signatures:

_____   _____

_____   _____

_____   _____

_____   _____

Directions: Read each statement below. Check only the statement or statements that apply to the student at the present time. Complete the form summary that follows based on the responses.

_____ The student's educational needs can be met in the regular education classroom with mild modifications to the instructional program.

_____ The regular education environment will impede the learning of the student.

_____ The student possesses the foundation or prerequisite academic skills necessary to be successful in the regular classroom.

_____ The student possesses the social skills necessary to foster healthy peer relationships.

_____ The student demonstrates frequent on-task behavior.

_____ The student demonstrates adequate study skills.

_____ The student can follow classroom rules and understands the consequence of misbehavior.

_____ The student possesses a desire to be with nondisabled students.

_____ The student's behavior in the regular education classroom will not impair the education of the nondisabled student.

Summary

_____ The student would benefit from an inclusive setting for academic instruction.
Circle recommendations: Reading   English   Math   Science   Social Studies
Other: _____

_____ The student would benefit from an inclusive setting for nonacademic activities.
Circle recommendations: Recess   Lunch   Assemblies   Clubs   Music
Art   Computer   Other: _____

_____ The student would not benefit from an inclusive setting at this time.

Team Comments: _____

_____

_____

Shelton, C. F., and Pollingue, A. B. *The Exceptional Teacher's Handbook: The First-Year Special Education Teacher's Guide for Success.* ©2000. Corwin Press, Inc.

Form 3.2   Teacher summary report

_____

Student name: _____   Date: _____

Teacher: _____

Class: _____

Period: _____

Directions: Please describe in detail how the student interacts and performs in your
                    classroom on an average basis. The information will be used by the IEP team
                    to facilitate the decision-making process in terms of selecting appropriate
                    inclusive settings for the student.

_____

_____

_____

_____

_____

_____

_____

_____

_____

_____

_____

_____

_____

_____

_____

Please return to: _____

Due date: _____

Shelton, C. F., and Pollingue, A. B. *The Exceptional Teacher's Handbook: The First-Year Special Education Teacher's Guide for Success.* ©2000. Corwin Press, Inc.

Step 2: Classroom Modifications

The development of appropriate classroom modifications is essential to the success of the student with exceptionalities in the regular classroom. After the decision to place the student in the inclusive setting is finalized, the IEP team must design and select modifications based on the student's identified deficit or deficits. A copy of the agreed-upon classroom modifications must be given to all inclusive teachers. The authors have included a selection of classroom strategies at the end of this section. The special education teacher can attach this information to the student's classroom modifications and distribute it to the appropriate regular education teachers. The following forms are presented in this section:

Form 3.3   Classroom modifications

Student Name: _____   Date: _____

Grade: _____   Subject: _____   Period: _____

Regular education teacher: _____

Special education teacher: _____

Note: The classroom modifications checked below must be implemented in order for
the student to experience success in his or her inclusive class or classes. The
modifications selected are in compliance with the student's individualized
educational program. In addition, the modifications are appropriate based on the
student's identified and documented learning deficits.

_____   Preferential seating
_____   Modified test (circle):
     - Oral test
     - Divide test into sections and utilize color-coding on matching test.
     - Open book test
     - Shortened test
     - Eliminate choices on multiple choice test
     - Extended time to complete test
     - Test may be read to student
_____   Student may leave class for resource assistance (this must be arranged in
     advance).
_____   Modified assignments (circle):
     - Shortened assignments (fewer math problems, fewer pages to read, and so on).
     - Extended time for assignment completion.
     - Allow student to utilize several alternatives to obtain information for reports:
     tapes, interviews, reading, experience, or making something, and so on.
_____   Assignment book
_____   Note-taking assistance
_____   Recognize and give credit for student's oral participation in class.
_____   Utilize cross-age tutoring.
_____   Avoid placing student under pressure of time or competition.
_____   Written assignments may be typed.
_____   Student may utilize cursive or manuscript writing.
_____   Give directions verbally and in written form.
_____   Utilize a behavior point system.
_____   Quietly repeat directions to student.
_____   Taped text/lectures.
_____   Special equipment needed or other recommended modifications (list):
_____   Mark student's correct and acceptable work only.
_____   Praise or reward student for appropriate behavior.

_____

_____

Form 3.4 Classroom modifications evaluation

Student Name: _____

Inclusive Class: _____

Regular Education Teacher: _____

Date: _____

Period: _____

Directions: List the interventions or adaptations that were implemented in the regular education environment in order to meet the needs of the inclusive student. Record and discuss the results of each and utilize the comments section to note all pertinent information.

Start Date	End Date	Intervention or adaptation strategies	Results	Comments

Shelton, C. F., and Pollingue, A. B. *The Exceptional Teacher's Handbook: The First-Year Special Education Teacher's Guide for Success.* ©2000. Corwin Press, Inc.

Form 3.5 Teacher suggestions for test modification

Test Description	Required Student Skills *Arlington County Public Schools, 1999	Suggested Test Modifications
Computation	*Possess content knowledge *Read at test vocabulary level *Possess the visual perceptual skills necessary to read and place the numbers in the correct order and space *Demonstrate good organizational skills *Possess legible penmanship	-Extended time for completion -Utilize graphing paper or ruler -Utilize calculator
Essay/Short Answer	*Possess content knowledge *Possess the ability to process a large quantity of material *Possess good writing skills and legible penmanship *Demonstrates good memory skills *Read at test vocabulary level *Possess an excellent vocabulary *Demonstrates good organizational and conceptual skills	-Extended time for completion -Read test to student -Rephrase/Restate question -Utilize word processing program (computer)
Fill In The Blank	*Possess content knowledge *Possess good writing skills *Possess the ability to copy the answers *Read at test vocabulary level *Possess good memory skills	-Extended time for completion -Provided a word bank -Read test to student
Matching	*Possess content knowledge *Possess ability to visually track test items *Read at test vocabulary level *Possess ability to discriminate figure from ground	-Extended time for completion -Read test to student -Divide test into sections and color-code each section and possible choices
Multiple Choice	*Possess content knowledge *Possess the ability to copy the answers or have the necessary visual perceptual skills to circle a letter/number or to transfer that letter/number to a separate paper *Read at test vocabulary level	-Extended time for completion -Eliminate a possible answer (choice) for each question -Read test to student
True/False	*Possess content knowledge *Possess the ability to discriminate inclusive vocabulary from exclusive vocabulary *Possess legible penmanship *Read at test vocabulary level	-Extended time for completion -Read test to student -Allow student to highlight key words such as "all," "never," and "never."

Shelton, C. F., and Pollingue, A. B. *The Exceptional Teacher's Handbook: The First-Year Special Education Teacher's Guide for Success.* ©2000. Corwin Press, Inc.

Form 3.6   The inclusive student's materials list

Student name: _____   Date: _____

The items checked below are recommended for your regular education class or classes:

_____ Three-ring binder with subject dividers	Additional Materials:
_____ Trapper Keeper™	_____
_____ Pencils	_____
_____ Ink pens	_____
_____ Assignment book	_____
_____ Paper	_____
_____ Pocket folders	_____
_____ Book bag	_____
_____ Calculator	_____
_____ Math compass	_____
_____ Graph paper	_____
_____ Glue	_____
_____ Scissors	_____
_____ Crayons	_____
_____ Color markers	_____
_____ Colored pencils	_____
_____ Index cards	_____
_____ Spiral notebook	_____

Parent signature: _____

Date: _____

Shelton, C. F., and Pollingue, A. B. *The Exceptional Teacher's Handbook: The First-Year Special Education Teacher's Guide for Success.* ©2000. Corwin Press, Inc.

Tips for the Regular Education Teacher

The authors have selected six disabilities recognized in the current regulations in the *Individuals with Disabilities Act* and provide recommended educational strategies for each disability. Special and regular education teachers can utilize the strategies in this section. This section provides tips for teachers of

- Specific learning disabilities students
- Behavioral disordered students
- Other health impaired students
- Attention deficit disordered students
- Hearing impaired students (mild to moderate hearing losses)
- Speech and language impaired students

Tips for Teachers of Specific Learning Disabilities Students

Following are tips for those who teach students with specific learning disabilities:

- Preferential Seating. The student should sit in a location that is free from distractions and in close proximity to the instructor.
- Write all homework or class assignments on the board.
- Utilize peer tutoring or peer helping. The peer tutor or helper can assist the student in the following manner:
  - Making certain they understand directions of assignments.
  - Reading important directions and essential material to them.
  - Drilling them orally on what they need to know.
  - Orally summarizing important textbook passages for the student.
  - Working with them in joint assignments.
  - Critiquing the student's work and making suggestions for improvement.
- Utilize a multisensory approach to instruction when possible.
- Conference with student as much as possible in order to verify that the student understands the course material and all instructions.
- Give student several alternatives to obtain and report information: tapes, interviews, reading, experience, or making something, and so on.
- Give student shortened assignments.

- Set up a specific homework schedule or test schedule so the student will know what to expect.

- Allow the student to underline or highlight in his or her textbook.

- Encourage the student to utilize flashcards for vocabulary word review.

- Give positive reinforcement as often as possible.

- Modify tests or quizzes according to the student's IEP.

Tips for Teachers of Students with Behavioral Disorders

The following tips may be helpful for those who teach students with behavioral disorders:

- Establish clear rules for the class and post in highly visible location.

- Rules are most effective when they are

  - Few in number

  - Relatively short

  - Stated positively (for example, "Work quietly" rather than "Do not make noise")

  - Regularly reviewed with students (Rizzo and Zabel, 1988, p. 220)

- Reinforce individual students when they follow the rules.

- Ignore inappropriate behavior when possible.

- Ensure that the consequences for not following the rules are fair, realistic, and appropriate for the offense.

- Develop a "safe plan" for times when the student feels as though he or she is about to lose control (for example, may go to see the school counselor or stand in the hallway).

- Provide an environment that is structured.

- Post the class schedule or routine. The teacher should inform the student in advance of a changes to the class schedule.

- Contact the student's parents to report both positive and negative information equally.

- Maintain accurate records on classroom behavior. Contact parents if the student exhibits significant and drastic changes in behavior.

- Frequently praise the student.

- Assign the student room responsibilities that will promote self-confidence.

Tips for Teachers of Other Health Impaired Students*

The following are tips for teachers working with students whose health is impaired:

- Be alert to signs of fatigue in the child.
- Find teaching materials that can be adapted to the physical needs of the student.
- Use teaching materials and activities that are appropriate for the age of the student.
- Make sure that all areas of the room and school are accessible.
- Make sure materials, projects, or leisure activities are within the student's reach.
- Encourage personal privacy when assisting the student with hygiene.
- Include activities each day that the student can accomplish from a wheelchair.
- Lift only as much weight as you can.
- Post emergency instructions and telephone numbers.

Tips for Teachers of ADD/ADHD Students

The following are tips for the those who teach students diagnosed with ADD/ADHD:

- Preferential Seating. The teacher should design a seating chart that will place the ADD/ADHD student in close proximity of instruction and away from areas of distraction.
- Classroom rules and consequences should be clear and concise and placed in a highly visible area.
- Present clear, specific, and simple directions in both written and oral form.
- Post the classroom schedule or routine.
- Avoid heavy doses of seat (sedentary) work.
- Provide an area in the room where the student can retreat when he or she is having a difficult time staying focused or controlling his or her activity level. Study carrels work great for elementary students.
- Provide the student with concrete activities and examples to demonstrate abstract concepts. Utilize hands-on and manipulative activities when possible.

---

*Smith and Luckasson, 1992, pp. 452.

- Utilize visual and verbal prompts and cues to maintain on-task behavior.
- Provide the student with opportunities to move around the room—running errands, helping in the classroom, handing out papers, cleaning the board, and so on.
- Positively reinforce appropriate behavior—immediately.
- Provide the student with a particular time frame for assignment completion. Assignments should be broken down into smaller pieces. Allow extended amount of time for assignment completion.
- Utilize medium intensity lighting.

Tips for Teachers of Hearing Impaired Students (Mild to Moderate Hearing Losses)

The following are tips for those who teach students who are hearing impaired:

- Talk facing the student.
- The student should sit close to the teacher or direction of instruction.
- The teacher should not stand in glaring light or with his or her back to an open window—this interferes with effective lip reading.
- If the student appears to be inattentive or not following your instruction, make certain that the student's hearing aid is turned on.
- The teacher should use complete but brief sentences during instruction.
- Reduce the background noise as much as possible.
- Articulate clearly, but do not talk louder unless you have an unusually soft voice.
- Make certain to have the student's attention before taking or starting a lesson.
- Speak normally. Do not over-enunciate words, speak louder than usual, or have forced facial expressions.
- Do not chew gum or cover you mouth when talking.
- Use visual aids whenever possible; an overhead projector is preferable to a blackboard.
- The teacher should familiarize the student with new vocabulary prior to introducing the new topic in class.
- Repeat and restate information by paraphrasing.

Tips for Teachers of Speech or Language Impaired Students*

The following are tips for the those who teach students whose speech or language abilities are impaired:

- Be alert to the presence of speech or language disorders.

- Refer children suspected of having a communicative disorder to an SLP.

- Remember that children with speech or language disorders have difficulty communicating with others.

- Work with the SLP to integrate appropriate language development activities in all academic instruction.

- Incorporate activities in class that allow children to practice skills mastered in therapy.

- Always consider the developmental stage of the child suspected of having a communicative disorder before making a referral.

- Create a supportive environment where children are encourage to communicate with each other.

- Create a section of the classroom where the physical environment—perhaps a large, round table—encourages sharing and discussion.

- Provide opportunities where children feel free to exchange ideas and discuss what they are learning in different subjects.

- Arrange for activities where children use oral language for different purposes (making a speech, leading a discussion) with different audiences (classmates, children in different classes).

- Build self-confidence in all children, particularly those with communicative disorders.

- Implement classroom adaptations in situations relying on class discussions, question/answer sessions, or student presentations on an as needed basis.

- Allow students with speech impairments to have an equal chance to voice their reactions or questions even if it means allowing extra time.

- The teacher should accept and respond to all of the student's appropriate attempts to communicate.

- The teacher should avoid interrupting or trying to complete the student's train of thought.   (The Office of Disability Resources, Bowling Green State University, May 2000 [On-line])

---

*Smith and Luckasson, 1992, pp. 191.

Step 3: Selecting Teachers for Inclusive Students

The process of selecting teachers for inclusive students is extremely difficult for most special education teachers. There are many regular education
teachers in our school systems who work wonderfully with disabled students. On the other hand, there are teachers that simply do not possess the
desire, teaching style, or instructional skills to meet the needs of special
students in the regular education classroom. The ultimate goal of most special educators is to identify colleagues who are amenable to working with
students with diverse learning abilities and styles. Most veteran special
education teachers have developed a system of selecting appropriate
teachers for students with disabilities. However, new teachers to the field
or school system view this task as extremely arduous. The authors suggest
three ways to begin the selection process. First, the new special education
teacher will often find that the most reliable sources of information are the
veteran special education teachers in their school. They will be able to
guide and assist the new teacher in his or her selection process. Secondly,
the special teacher can conduct a survey of the school's faculty members.
A non-intrusive, generic teacher survey is provided in this chapter. The
survey can be easily administered and interpreted. The results of the survey will lay the foundation for selecting appropriate regular education
teachers for students. Finally, the authors suggest that the new special education teacher seek advice from the principal or other administrative staff.
These people usually know the school's faculty and can assist the new
teacher in the selection process.

Section Forms

Form 3.7A   Regular education teacher survey

Directions:

The attached survey is designed to facilitate the process of selecting regular education teachers for students with disabilities. The results of the survey will assist the special education teacher in his or her effort to match teaching styles with students' learning styles. Please read each question carefully and place a check mark by the statements that accurately describe your teaching style, techniques, and philosophy. The results of the survey are confidential and will be maintained in a locked file cabinet for security.

Please return to: _____

Due date: _____

Form 3.7B   Regular education teacher survey

Date: _____

Teacher: _____   Grade: _____

Subject: _____

1. _____ The students have assigned seats and I maintain a seating chart.
2. _____ The students are allowed to sit in a location of their choice.
3. _____ The students are required to maintain an organized notebook.
4. _____ The students are given a list of required materials for the class.
5. _____ Classroom rules and consequences are posted in a highly visible location and have been discussed in detail with the students.
6. _____ The students are required to maintain an assignment book.
7. _____ I encourage the students to write down all assignments.
8. _____ I write all assignments on an assignment board or in a highly visible location.
9. _____ I give a weekly or unit syllabus to all students.
10. _____ Graded papers are returned immediately to the students.
11. _____ Graded papers are sent home once a week and a parent signature is required before returning papers to school.
12. _____ Students are frequently divided into cooperative learning groups for various classroom activities.
13. _____ Students are placed in groups only for the purpose of lab activities or major class projects.
14. _____ Students are required to take notes on a daily basis.
15. _____ Students are encouraged to take notes; however, I provide handouts that cover the key points of section, chapter, or unit.
16. _____ I utilize a lecture format as a primary means of instruction.
17. _____ I utilize a combination of lecture and discussion as a primary means of instruction.
18. _____ I utilize a combination of lecture, discussion, and hands-on activities as a primary format of instruction.
19. _____ My tests are strictly objective: multiple choice, fill-in-the-blank, or matching.
20. _____ My tests are strictly subjective: essay
21. _____ My tests are a combination of objective and subjective.
22. _____ I provide opportunities for remediation.
23. _____ Students are given weekly progress reports.
24. _____ Students are given progress reports or report cards as directed by the school system.
25. _____ Parents are notified when a student is not performing to his or her potential.
26. _____ I utilize technology in the classroom.
27. _____ I modify test or instructional materials to meet the needs of the students.
28. _____ I enjoy working with students from all backgrounds.
29. _____ I am firm and consistent with the classroom discipline policy.
30. _____ I am organized and structured in my approach to teaching.

Shelton, C. F., and Pollingue, A. B. *The Exceptional Teacher's Handbook: The First-Year Special Education Teacher's Guide for Success.* ©2000. Corwin Press, Inc.

Step 4: Monitoring Students

The special education teacher should monitor all students placed in regular education settings in order to address academic, behavior, or other problems before they escalate and affect educational performance. The authors have developed four forms that will assist the first-year teacher with the documentation and tracking of student progress.

The following forms are found in this section:

Form 3.8A   Exceptional student's monitor form

The special education teacher should periodically monitor all students placed in inclusive settings in order to address problems before they escalate and affect student performance. One of the most time-efficient methods of monitoring students is by way of a checklist. The authors have developed a monitor checklist for regular education teachers. This checklist can be quickly completed by the teachers and provides a total view of student performance in the regular education classroom. Please review the following directions before distributing the Exceptional Student Monitor form to teachers of inclusive students:

Directions:

1. Complete the top portion of monitor form and distribute to each teacher of the inclusive student.
2. Monitor forms should be given to each teacher at a minimum of every three weeks or between each official school reporting period.
3. Explain to each teacher that the information completed on the form will be shared with the student and the parent when appropriate.
4. After receiving a monitor form that indicates areas of concern, consult with the teacher as soon as possible.
5. Arrange conference as soon as possible when concerns are of significant magnitude.
6. Special education teachers should maintain a folder of all monitor forms for documentation purposes.
7. Monitor forms should be reviewed at the annual individualized education program team meeting.

Shelton, C. F., and Pollingue, A. B. *The Exceptional Teacher's Handbook: The First-Year Special Education Teacher's Guide for Success.* ©2000. Corwin Press, Inc.

Form 3.8B   Exceptional student's monitor form

Student: _____   Date: _____

Teacher: _____   Subject: _____

Note: The information recorded on this monitor form will be shared with the student
         and his or her parents when appropriate and filed for documentation.

Class participation: Pass: _____   Fail: _____

Class/daily work: Pass: _____   Fail: _____

Homework: Pass: _____   Fail: _____

Quiz grades: Pass: _____   Fail: _____

Test grades: Pass: _____   Fail: _____

On task behavior: Good: _____   Fair: _____   Poor: _____

Tardy/absent: T: _____   Ab: _____

Overall performance: Pass: _____   Fail: _____

Teacher request conference: Yes: _____   No: _____

Teacher concerns:

_____

_____

_____

Return form to: _____

Due date: _____

Shelton, C. F., and Pollingue, A. B. *The Exceptional Teacher's Handbook: The First-Year Special Education Teacher's Guide for Success.* ©2000. Corwin Press, Inc.

Form 3.9 Exceptional student's monitor results summary

Student name: _____

Report period: _____

Report date: _____

Note: This is to be utilized as a summary of the *Exceptional Student Monitor* form. The special education teacher should review each student's completed monitor forms and place check marks in problem areas. The summary form is a quick reference of the student's progress in his or her inclusive classes.

Subject	Class Participation	Class Work	Homework	Test Grades	On-Task Behavior	Overall Performance	Tardy	Absent

Shelton, C. F., and Pollingue, A. B. *The Exceptional Teacher's Handbook: The First-Year Special Education Teacher's Guide for Success.* ©2000. Corwin Press, Inc.

Form 3.10 Exceptional student's progress report summary

Report period: _____

Note: The special education teacher should record the grades of all students assigned to his or her caseload in their inclusive classes during the progress report time period. Schools usually issue a formal progress report halfway through each reporting period. The authors strongly recommend that the teacher highlight all subjects in which students receives a grade of "D" or "F."

Student Name	Language Arts	Mathematics	Science	Social Studies	Physical Education	Elective or Exploratory Courses

Shelton, C. F., and Pollingue, A. B. *The Exceptional Teacher's Handbook: The First-Year Special Education Teacher's Guide for Success.* ©2000. Corwin Press, Inc.

Form 3.11 Exceptional student's final grade summary

Student Name: _____   School Year: _____   Semester _____

Academic Subject	First Reporting Period Average	Second Reporting Period Average	Third Reporting Period Average	Semester Exam Grade	Days Absent	Conduct Average	Teacher's Comments

Additional Information: _____

Shelton, C. F., and Pollingue, A. B. *The Exceptional Teacher's Handbook: The First-Year Special Education Teacher's Guide for Success.*
©2000. Corwin Press, Inc.

Managing the Special Education Classroom

The special education classroom is often a place filled with a high level of activity throughout the school day. The authors recommend that the new teacher have a classroom management plan in place on the first day of school in order to promote a positive learning environment and prevent total chaos. The plan should reflect the basic educational philosophy of the teacher, be appropriate for the student population, and be approved by the school's principal. The inclusion of the components listed below will lay the foundation for an effective classroom management plan:

- Classroom policies and procedures that regulate all class activity.
- Effective approaches to discipline and behavior modification in the classroom.
- Procedures for communicating with students and parents throughout the school year.

The authors advise the new teacher to thoroughly explain and discuss classroom expectations with students as soon as possible. According to Harry Wong (1991), "Effective teachers spend a good deal of time the first weeks of the school year introducing, teaching, modeling, and practicing procedures until they become routines." (p. 1.)

In the pages that follow, the authors provide the first-year teacher with the necessary framework on which to build a solid classroom management plan. The authors have divided the chapter into three main sections, with each section addressing one of the above components. Supplemental forms and checklists are provided in order to assist and support the new special education teacher's formation of his or her first plan. The designing and implementing of a strong classroom management plan at the beginning of the school year will result most likely in a positive experience for students and the new teacher.

Section 1: Classroom Policies and Procedures

The establishing of policies and procedures is extremely important to the basic operation of the special education classroom. The new teacher should understand the difference between the two terms before developing his or her plan of action. Classroom procedures are designated methods for completing certain class activities or tasks. The teacher can think of classroom procedures as the way to "conduct business" in the classroom. Classroom policies are set of guiding principles or courses of action.

The new teacher should review the checklist of activities or issues on the following page and select the items that apply to his or her current teaching situation that require the development of a policy or procedure. The teacher can add items as needed at the end of the list.

Classroom Policies and Procedures Checklist

Directions: Check all student and teacher activities or issues that require the establishment of a classroom policy or procedure. Additional items can be added at the end of each list.

Classroom Procedures Are Needed for

_____ How students are to enter the classroom

_____ How students are to exit the classroom

_____ How and when students will be excused to the restroom

_____ How and when students will get a drink of water

_____ Class schedule for academics or specialty classes

_____ How students are to respond or ask questions in the classroom

_____ How and when will students move around in the classroom

_____ Specify appropriate student behavior when working with other students

_____ Where are students to place personal items (book bags, coats, lunch boxes, and so on)

_____ How teacher will collect monies (lunch, field trip, book fines, and so on)

_____ How students are to move in the hallway

_____ Other: _____

_____

Classroom Procedures Are Needed for

_____ Grading System or method

_____ Late work

_____ Class work

_____ Make-up work

_____ Homework

_____ Student tardiness

_____ Student attendance

_____ Reporting student progress

_____ Reporting student final grade

_____ Required class materials

_____ Assessment of students in the special and inclusive classroom

_____ Other: _____

_____

_____

_____

_____

Section 2: Classroom Discipline and Behavior Management

Several approaches to classroom discipline may be used. The new teacher must select the approach that does not conflict with his or her educational philosophy and fits the need of the educational program. A large majority of both regular and special education teachers utilize some aspect of the *Assertive Discipline Approach* developed by Lee and Marlene Canter. The establishment and implementation of classroom rules and consequences and recognition of students for following the rules of the class are both a part of the assertive discipline model. Another discipline model special education teachers frequently utilize is the *Behavior Analysis Model.* "The key to this model is the use of reinforcers, both positive and negative, to obtain desired behavior and to extinguish inappropriate behavior" (Koorland, 1995, p. 149). The authors have found this approach to be effective in changing behavior in students with disabilities.

The authors recommend that the first-year special education teacher develop a classroom discipline plan prior to the start of the school year. Guidelines for developing rules and consequences and behavior management plans are included in this section. The new teacher should obtain approval of discipline plans and behavior modification strategies prior to implementation.

Classroom Rules

- Rules should be few in number: One to five is plenty.
- Rules should be positively stated ("Work quietly" versus "Don't talk").
- Rules should be appropriate for the age and disability of the student.
- Rules should fall within the school guidelines (include school rules).

Classroom Consequences

- Consequences must be appropriate for infraction.
- Consequences must be enforced consistently and as immediately as possible.
- "Consequences should be listed in a discipline hierarchy," (Canter, 1995, p. 257); for example, warning, first offense, second offense, and so on.

Positive Recognition

Canter (1995) states that "positive recognition will motivate students to follow rules that the teacher creates" (p. 255).

- Verbal praise
- Positive notes home
- Telephone calls home

- Special privileges
- Certificates and awards
- Tangible rewards

Behavior Modification Plans

- Clearly identify the target behavior (the behavior to be changed).
- Collect information on when the behavior occurs and under what conditions.
- Write a behavioral objective.
- Implement reinforcer and chart effectiveness.
- Vary the reinforcement schedule and chart results.
- Stop the reinforcer and evaluate student behavior.

Section 3: Communicating with Students and Parents

The first-year special education teacher should include procedures for communicating with students and parents in his or her classroom management plan. Communication can be in the form of a note, telephone call, home visit, or a parent-teacher conference. The new teacher should remember that good communication between school and home will foster the parent-teacher relationship.

Suggestions for Communicating with Parents and Students

- Teacher-student conference
- Parent-teacher conference
- Telephone conference with parent
- Home visit with parent
- Letter to parent
- Notes to students
- Class meetings
- Positive sticker on a good paper
- Weekly progress report
- Daily progress report

Chapter 4: Supplemental Forms

Form 4.1   Daily point system

Week of: _____

Class: _____   Period: _____

Directions: List the names of the students in your class. Place check marks when a
student exhibits a behavior listed. The results can be used as part of a reward
system established by the classroom teacher.

Classroom Behaviors

Student Name	On Time to Class	Prepared For Class: 1. Pencil 2. Paper 3. Homework 4. Textbook 5. Notebook	Works Quietly in Class	Stays On Task	Participates In Class	TOTAL

Shelton, C. F., and Pollingue, A. B. *The Exceptional Teacher's Handbook: The First-Year Special Education Teacher's Guide for Success.* ©2000. Corwin Press, Inc.

Form 4.2 Classroom detention

> **Classroom Detention**
>
> Student: _____
>
> Grade: _____
>
> Date and time of detention: _____
>
> Teacher assigning detention: _____
>
> Reason for detention:
>
> _____
>
> _____
>
> _____
>
> _____
>
> Parent signature: _____

Form 4.3 Hall pass

Hall Pass

Date: _____

Student name: _____

Destination (circle):

        Main office
        Media center
        Restroom
        Water fountain
        Classroom: _____
        Other: _____

Time departed: _____

Time arrived: _____

Teacher signature: _____

Form 4.4   Student progress report

Student Name:_____   Date:_____

Directions: Please check the column that accurately depicts the student's progress in the
subject and behavior columns and provide comments where necessary.

Subject/Behavior	Satisfactory	Needs Improvement
Reading		
English		
Math		
Science		
Social Studies		
Written expression		
Follows class rules		
Exhibits courteous behavior		
Respects personal and school property		
Participates in class		
Completes assigned work		
Follows directions		
Brings materials to class		

Parent signature: _____

Shelton, C. F., and Pollingue, A. B. *The Exceptional Teacher's Handbook: The First-Year Special Education Teacher's Guide for Success.* ©2000. Corwin Press, Inc.

5

Planning Academic Instruction for Students with Disabilities

The teaching of students with disabilities is a monumental task that requires a tremendous amount of preparation. The authors identify five basic steps involved in the instructional planning process. First, the teacher must review each student's IEP and identify the academic goals and objectives that must be addressed during the school year. The individualized education plan is the foundation and driving force behind all academic instruction in the special education classroom. Secondly, the instructor should review and select instructional materials that are appropriate for students with disabilities and support the curriculum for the designated subject or skill areas. The authors strongly recommend that the new teacher use the instructional materials available in his or her school system. However, in the event that these materials are not appropriate, the authors suggest that the teacher purchase non-consumable materials when possible. Third, the new teacher should create a class schedule that will accommodate academic instruction, students in inclusive classes, specialty, exploratory, or elective classes, lunch, and recess (when appropriate). Next, the new teacher should design a classroom that will promote and enhance the learning experience. Classroom design involves the physical arrangement of the classroom, bulletin boards, and color schemes. Finally, the first-year special education teacher should plan and develop lesson plans that consider how the student receives and processes information, address the need of the student, and promote a sense of wonder and excitement within the student. The completion of these steps should maximize student performance and teacher effectiveness.

In Chapter 5, the authors provide the new teacher with information that will lay the groundwork for a successful teaching experience. The authors have included checklists, forms, and teacher tips that will assist the teacher through each step of the planning process.

Section 1: IEP Goals and Objectives

In the special education classroom, instruction is based on the goals and objectives in each student's individualized education plan. The first-year teacher must review each student's IEP and identify the following information before forming and implementing instructional plans:

- Specific skills to be taught
- Specific methods and materials to be utilized in the instruction process
- A specified method of evaluating each objective
- Initiation and completion dates
- Listing of service provider

In Section 1, the authors provide an **IEP Goals and Objectives Checklist** (Form 5.1) designed to assist the new special education teacher with instructional planning. After completing the checklist, the teacher should be able to chart out his or her direction for academic instruction for the school year, collect or purchase appropriate instructional materials, and complete lesson plans that incorporate the instructional and evaluation methods recommended for each student.

Section 1 Forms

This section contains the following forms:

Form 5.1 IEP goals and objectives checklist

Student Name: _____

School Year: _____

Directions: Complete the information below upon review of each student's individualized education program.

Skill Area	Instructional Methods	Required Instructional Materials	Methods of Evaluation

Skill Area: Academic, Social, Daily Living, Leisure, Transition, or Other.

Instructional Method: Modeling, Guided Practice, Reinforcements, drill and practice, use of manipulative, chaining, whole language approach, direct instruction, learning strategies, multisensory approach, or other.

Instructional Materials: Textbooks, Supporting Materials, Manipulatives, Concrete Materials, or other.

Methods of Evaluation: Observation, Work Sample, Unit Tests, Surveys, Interviews, Criterion-reference Tests, or other.

Shelton, C. F., and Pollingue, A. B. *The Exceptional Teacher's Handbook: The First-Year Special Education Teacher's Guide for Success.* ©2000. Corwin Press, Inc.

Section 2: Selecting Instructional Materials

The special education teacher must begin the process of selecting instructional materials after the review of each student's IEP has been completed. For the inexperienced teacher, the selection process can seem somewhat overwhelming and confusing. Mercer and Mercer (1993) suggest that teachers utilize the following plan when selecting instructional materials:

1. Identify the curriculum areas in which materials are needed.

2. Rank the areas from highest to lowest priority.

3. List affordable materials that are designed to teach the selected skill area or areas.

4. Obtain the materials and evaluate them so a decision can be made regarding a purchase. On request, many publishers will provide a sample of materials or a manual for the teacher to examine or field test. Also, many school districts have resource or curriculum centers that contain materials for teachers to inspect (p. 150).

In addition, the new teacher can consult with other special education teachers on staff for advice and guidance. The authors have provided a list of commercial publishers in Appendix E of this handbook.

Section 2 Forms

The following forms are found in this section:

Form 5.2   Classroom teacher's instructional materials list

Teacher Name: _____   Date: _____

Program: _____   Room: _____

Skill Area	Instructional Materials: List and Describe	Quantity Requested	Company Name, Address, and Telephone Number

Section 3: Creating a Class Schedule

An effective class schedule is vital to the overall operation of the special education classroom. The class schedule provides class structure, ensures that instruction time for the core academic areas is maximized, and integrates lower priority classes with other miscellaneous activities. Class schedules vary greatly among the various special education programs and between the different grade levels. The special education teacher should design a class schedule that flows with the school's master schedule, is conducive to the schedules of inclusive students, and allows for teacher planning. The authors list some suggestions for class schedules based on grade level.

Elementary Level*

- Analyze the day's events
- Plan opening exercises
- Schedule academic instruction
- Plan closing exercises

Secondary Level

- Homeroom
- Academic instruction: school day is divided into class periods (Possibly 6-7 classes a day/50-55 minutes per class)
- Lunch
- Exploratory class (middle school)
- Elective class (high school)
- Transition program
- Planning
- Advisement

Section 4 Forms

The following forms are found in this section:

---

*(Mercer & Mercer, 1993, p. 128)

Form 5.3 Class schedule

Teacher: _____

Semester: _____

School Year: _____

Time	Subject/Activity
—	
—	
—	
—	
—	
—	

Shelton, C. F., and Pollingue, A. B. *The Exceptional Teacher's Handbook: The First-Year Special Education Teacher's Guide for Success.*
©2000. Corwin Press, Inc.

Section 4: Tips for Classroom Designs, Color Schemes, and Bulletin Boards

The first-year special education teacher should consider several aspects of classroom layout, use of color, and bulletin board design when planning his or her classroom.

Classroom Design Components

- Main instruction area
- Small group instruction area
- Learning centers area
- Computer or technology area
- Free reading area
- Reference book area
- Teacher instructional materials area
- Student materials area
- Independent study area
- Teacher desk area
- Paraprofessional desk area
- Listening Center
- Teacher storage area

Color Schemes in the Special Education Classroom

- Colors that contrast one another on the color wheel are stimulating in nature (for example, blue and orange).
- Colors that are next to one another on the color wheel are calming in nature (for example, peach and rose).

Bulletin Boards in the Special Education Classroom

- Bulletin boards can be used for a variety of purposes
    - Display student work (neatly)
    - Posting of school news
    - Extension of instructional unit or theme
    - Aid in instruction/reinforce skill
    - Posting notices
    - Decorating the classroom
- Commercial or teacher-made materials can be used
- Materials should be laminated for durability

- Make a titles for bulletin board to explain theme or purpose
- Use contrasting colors
- Bulletin boards are appropriate for all age groups
- Designate a storage place for all bulletin board materials

Section 5: Tips for Instructional Planning and Implementation

This section provides some hints for better lesson planning and implementation.

Instructional Planning Guide

- Plan lessons *at least* one week in advance.
- Set aside time each day to plan—don't try to do all your planning in one day.
- Select objectives for each lesson to be taught.
- Write objectives on the board or post in highly visible location.
- Select supporting materials to reinforce lesson objectives or skills being taught.
- Make copies of all worksheets in advance.
- Write all plans in a lesson plan book or in the format required by your school.
- Give a copy of your lesson plans to the designated person at your school.
- Secure all additional materials for the lesson in advance (for example, videos, maps, and calculators).
- Prepare a weekly syllabus or homework calendar for students.
- Inform students in advance of all tests dates.
- Make sure overhead projector or other piece of equipment is in working order in advance of lesson presentation.
- Review all lessons prior to class period.

Implementation of Lesson Plans

- Introduce lesson or skill—create a sense of wonder in the student
- Pre-teach lesson vocabulary
- Pre-test when appropriate
- Demonstrate skill: Explain and discuss with students
- Provide opportunity for guided practice: Correct and discuss
- Provide opportunity for independent practice: Correct and discuss
- Check on learning

- Re-teach problem areas
- Evaluation of skill mastery

Section 5 Forms

The following forms are found in this section:

Form 5.4 Weekly lesson plan

Class/Subject: _____   Week of: _____

Class Time: _____   Period: _____

Textbook: _____

Class Roster: _____

_____

Chapter/Topic: _____

Lesson Objectives: _____

_____

Day	Activities/Content	Homework
Monday Date:		
Tuesday Date:		
Wednesday Date:		
Thursday Date:		
Friday Date:		

Shelton, C. F., and Pollingue, A. B. *The Exceptional Teacher's Handbook: The First-Year Special Education Teacher's Guide for Success.*
©2000. Corwin Press, Inc.

Preparing for a Successful Parent-Teacher Conference

6

The first-year special education teacher must establish and maintain communication with the parents of his or her assigned students throughout the school year. A majority of the time it is appropriate for the communication to take the form of a telephone call or a note home. However, some situations dictate a face-to-face conference between teacher and parent. Kroth and Simpson (1977) state that "The parent-teacher conference is an individualized, personalized meeting between two or three significant persons in the child's life with the purpose of accelerating his or her growth" (p. 2). The parent-teacher conference is an excellent opportunity to develop rapport with parents. If the new teacher utilizes good conferencing skills, not only will rapport be established, but the foundation will be laid for a good parent-teacher relationship. Parent-teacher conferences tend to be more personal, productive, and provide a less chance for the misinterpretation of information.

The objectives of a parent-teacher conference depend on the purpose of the meeting. The following is a list of conference categories most frequently utilized by the special education teacher: progress report, problem-solving, and the mandated individualized education program annual review meeting. In each type of conference, the special education teacher must exercise good listening skills. Parents need to leave each conference with the feeling that someone truly understands their concerns and feel confident that the plans developed will be implemented. The parent-teacher conference requires a tremendous amount of prior planning on behalf of the special education teacher. The authors have developed a recommended checklist for each type of conference to assist the special education teacher in his or her conference preparation and ensure a successful and productive parent-teacher meeting. Furthermore, the authors have included an additional list of tasks that generally contribute to the success of most conferences. The tasks are arranged in the following fashion:

- Pre-conference tasks

- Tasks throughout conference

- Post-conference tasks

Finally, the teacher of students with disabilities must remember that communication does not flow in only one direction. It is just as imperative for the teacher to disseminate information as to acquire it. Special education teachers must maintain an open line of communication with the parents of his or her special needs students.

Essential Tasks for All Parent-Teacher Conferences

Pre-Conference Tasks

_____ Prior written notification of meeting given to the parents and other conference participants (at least 7 to 10 working days in advance).

_____ Notification of meeting should include the following (Form 6.1):

    a. Date, time, and exact location of conference.

    b. Purpose of conference.

    c. List of persons and their respective positions to attend conference. (Include parent and student's name in notification. It is mandatory that a student with a disability of any age be invited if the purpose of the meeting is to consider or discuss transition services.)

    d. Request confirmation of attendance from all invitees.

    e. List special education teacher's name and telephone number as contact person for all conference inquiries.

_____ Select and reserve conference location. This location needs to be in a neutral area that is comfortable and free from interruptions such as the school's main conference room or media center's conference room.

_____ Formulate a meeting agenda and distribute to parents and all school personnel invited to conference before the designated meeting date.

_____ Send parents a conference preparation handout (Form 6.2) (Shea and Bauer, 1991, p. 146).

_____ Telephone parents two days prior to conference as a friendly reminder.

_____ Confirm conference with school personnel two days prior to conference (Form 6.3, Friendly Reminder).

_____ Ensure the following school personnel have been invited to these conferences:

    a. Progress report conference: parents, regular education teachers of inclusive students, school counselor, special education teacher, and additional special education staff

    b. Problem-solving conference: parents, school administrator, regular education teachers of inclusive students, school counselor, special education coordinator or support person, special education teacher, and additional special education staff

    c. IEP conference: parents, at least one regular education teacher of inclusive students, at least one special education teacher, school or special education administrator, related services, transition service participants, and the student (if appropriate)

Tasks to Complete Throughout Conference

_____ Introduce school principal, faculty, and special education personnel to parents.

_____ Give Parent Rights booklet to the parents when appropriate.

_____ State the purpose of the conference.

_____ The special education teacher or the appointee should take copious notes during the meeting and highlight all significant information (Form 6.4).

_____ The special education teacher should close the conference by summarizing all information discussed and review any additions to the student's IEP.

_____ All information discussed and plans developed during the meeting should be written on a minutes form and signed by all people attending the conference.

_____ Give parents a copy of the conference minutes.

Post-Conference Tasks

_____ Send parents a follow-up letter that includes the following (Form 6.5):

Thank parents for attending the meeting.

Send any documents requested to the parents.

Send the best school hours and days to reach special education teacher if parents have further questions.

Conclude letter with positive comment about the student.

Essential Information for the Progress Report Conference

Note: The following information must be collected and reviewed by the special education teacher prior to the progress report conference.

General Student Information

_____ Current student school attendance record:

Request a copy of the student's attendance record from your school's attendance office.

Review the student's tardy record.

Request that all inclusive teachers note attendance and tardy information on student's monitor form (See Chapters 1 and 3).

_____ Current student school discipline record:

Request a summary report of the student's discipline record from the school's discipline office or the student's discipline administrator.

Review the student's discipline record for the following:
   a. Description of discipline referrals or classroom infractions.
   b. Discipline referrals date and time.
   c. Name of referring school official.

_____ Review student's academic school record with the school counselor:

Review last year's academic achievements.

Review the total number of earned high school units/credits.*

Review the program of study or academic emphasis the student has decided to pursue.*

General Classroom Information

_____ Review information from regular education teachers for students in inclusive settings:

Class participation

Class/daily work

Quiz grades

Test grades

On-task behavior

Tardy/absent

Overall performance

---

*This information is relevant for high school students only.

_____ Review information from special education teacher:

    a.   Current mastery of IEP objectives.

    b.   Current successful instructional strategies.

    c.   Current successful behavior modification strategies.

    d.   Status on previously developed plans or strategies.

    e.   Overall performance in the special education classroom.

Essential Information for the Problem-Solving Conference

Note: The following information must be collected and reviewed by the special education teacher prior to the problem-solving conference.

Identify Present Student Problem

A. Behavior problem:

Problem involves:

1. Student self-control

2. Student affect: enthusiasm, leadership, followership, responsibility, reactions to rewards and contingencies

3. Social conventions: manners, courtesy, respect for others and their property

Problem occurs:

1. Special education classroom or setting

2. Regular education classroom or setting

3. Recess

4. Field trips

5. School bus

6. Bathroom

7. Hallway

8. Lunchroom

B. Academic problem:

Problem involves:

1. Student's performance in the area or areas of reading, spelling, English, science, social studies, math, other

2. Student's performance on tests

3. Student's performance on quizzes

4. Student's homework completion

5. Student's completion of assigned projects

Problem occurs:

1. Regular education classroom or setting

Class: _____

Teacher: _____

2. Special education classroom or setting

Class: _____

Teacher: _____

Essential Information for the Individualized Education Program Conference

Note: The following information must be collected and reviewed by the special education teacher prior to the individualized education program conference.

_____ Review current levels of performance:

1. Educational assessments
   a. Intelligence
   b. Academic achievement
   c. Learning style
   d. Adaptive behavior
   e. Social/emotional
   f. Fine and gross motor
2. Audiological assessment
3. Speech/language pathologist assessment
4. Physical therapy assessment
5. Occupational therapy assessment
6. Fine and gross motor skills assessment
7. Current medical status

_____ Review current individualized education program:

1. Goals and objectives (annotate the mastered goals and objectives on current IEP)
2. Related services: transportation, physical therapy, occupational therapy, speech and language therapy, other
3. Student's current placement:
   _____ Regular class
   _____ Resource class
   _____ Separate/self-contained class
   _____ Public separate school facility
   _____ Private separate school facility
   _____ Public residential facility
   _____ Private residential facility
   _____ Homebound/hospital environment
4. Student's discipline plan
5. Student's behavior management plan
6. Student's standardized testing modifications
7. Student's transition plan

_____ Review student's performance in regular education classes

_____ Test grades   _____ Quiz grades   _____ Homework completion
_____ Class participation   _____ On-task behavior   _____ Conduct

_____ Review general student information:

1. Attendance record
2. Discipline record
3. School transcript (high school students only)
4. Student program of study (high school students only)

Chapter 6: Supplemental Forms

Form 6.1   Conference notification

Date: _____

Student Name: _____   Grade: _____

Conference Date and Time: _____

Location: _____

Conference Participants:

_____

_____

_____

_____

Conference purpose:_____

_____

_____

_____

_____

_____

_____

_____

_____

Information requested:

_____ Attendance   _____ Test grades

_____ Tardy   _____ Quiz grades

_____ Discipline   _____ On-task behavior

_____ Other:_____

_____

_____

Form 6.2   Parent handout for conference preparation*

Before the conference:

1.   Make arrangements for your other children, if necessary. The conference is for you and your child's teacher; small children can be distracting and take time away from the discussion.

2.   Jot down any questions you may have for the teacher, such as
         - Is my child working to the best of his (her) ability?
         - How is he (or she) progressing in reading, math, handwriting, and other subjects?
         - Does he (or she) get along well with teachers, children?
         - Does he (or she) follow classroom rules?
         - What is his (or her) attitude in class?
         - How do you handle (specific behaviors)?
         - What do the tests say about his (or her) ability?

3.   Talk to your child about the conference. Ask if he or she wants you to ask any questions or voice any concerns.

4.   Collect any records or information that may help the teacher. Try to anticipate questions and prepare answers.

At the conference:

1.   Please be on time and stay only for your scheduled time. You may schedule another conference if you do not cover all the necessary information in the allotted time.

2.   Discuss only the child at issue. Try not to stray off the subject. Do not bring up your other children's problems.

3.   Ask any questions about your child's education. Advocate for your child. Know your child's and your rights.

4.   Volunteer information that may help the teacher plan programming for your child.

5.   Feel free to take notes to review later.

After the conference, feel free to contact your child's teacher for further clarification.

Shelton, C. F., and Pollingue, A. B. *The Exceptional Teacher's Handbook: The First-Year Special Education Teacher's Guide for Success.* ©2000. Corwin Press, Inc.
*Shea and Bauer, 1991, p.146.

Form 6.3   Conference reminder

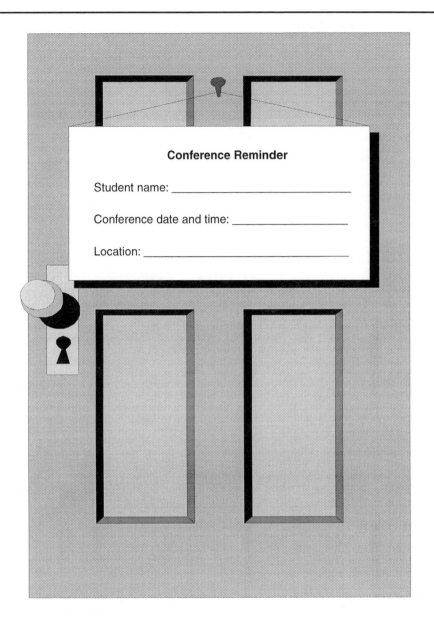

Conference Reminder

Student name: _____

Conference date and time: _____

Location: _____

Shelton, C. F., and Pollingue, A. B. *The Exceptional Teacher's Handbook: The First-Year Special Education Teacher's Guide for Success.* ©2000. Corwin Press, Inc.

Form 6.4   Conference minutes

Date: _____

Student Name: _____   Grade: _____

Disability: _____   Placement: _____

Conference Purpose:

_____
_____
_____
_____
_____
_____
_____

Conference Summary:

_____
_____
_____
_____
_____
_____
_____
_____
_____
_____
_____
_____
_____
_____
_____
_____

Conference Participants:

_____   _____   _____

_____   _____   _____

_____   _____   _____

Form 6.5   Conference summary

Date: _____

Dear _____:

_____

_____

_____

_____

_____

_____

_____

_____

_____

_____

_____

_____

_____

_____

_____

Sincerely,

Enclosures

_____ Meeting minutes   _____ IEP documents

_____ Behavior contracts   _____ Academic strategies

_____ Behavior strategies   _____ Other

7

Understanding
Educational Assessments

The special education teacher will be required to review thousands of student educational assessments over the course of his or her career. Professionals in the field of special education should be familiar with the various tests that are administered to students with disabilities and be able to independently analyze the results of those tests. Frequently, special education teachers become dependent on the school psychologist to interpret every aspect of a student's educational assessment. However, it is imperative that the special education teacher be able to review all tests administered to students and independently interpret the results of those tests. The premise for this requirement is that it is the special education teacher who must utilize the results of these assessments for the purpose of planning and implementing appropriate individualized educational program plans.

In the pages that follow, the authors provide the new teacher with a review of the three main levels of assessment; basic test and measurement information; a test administration preparation guideline; and a description of the educational assessments the new teacher is most likely to encounter during his or her first year. After reviewing the information in this chapter, the new teacher should be able to administer and interpret educational assessments with precision and confidence.

Levels of Educational Assessment

Most students with disabilities undergo a variety of educational assessments at various levels before being placed in a designated special education program. The first level of assessment typically begins in the regular classroom. The regular education teacher identifies a student who consistently fails to perform academically or exhibits frequent inappropriate behavior. The special education teacher can be asked to review student's work samples or complete a classroom observation. The new special education teacher should be able to determine if there is a substantial amount of evidence to refer the student for diagnostic testing. Diagnostic testing is usually the second level of educational assessment. The school counselor or special education teacher can be responsible for specific diagnostic testing at the school level. The student should be referred to the third assessment level if the diagnostic assessments continue to identify deficit or problem areas. At third level, a license school psychologist usually conducts a comprehensive educational assessment. A battery of tests are administered to the student in order to measure the student's intellectual aptitudes, academic achievement, acuity, and learning style. In addition, classroom observations are conducted to document how the student functions both academically, behaviorally, and socially in the classroom. Student work samples are collected from the classroom teacher. An adaptive behavior scale is usually completed if the student is suspected of being intellectually disabled. For initial referrals, the parents complete an in-depth developmental and medical history. The student's permanent school record is reviewed. The school psychologist compiles all test results (formal and informal), observations, work samples, parent and school history information and completes the final assessment report. The report is presented to a team of educators, the student's parents, and the student (when appropriate), and the results are explained and discussed at great length. This report is the basis for student placement and individualized educational program planning.

Basic Test and Measurement Information

I. Standardized Tests

These test are commercially prepared by experts in measurement and subject matter. They provide methods for obtaining samples of behavior under uniform procedures. Scoring is usually objective. Usually a standardized test has been administered to a norm group (or groups) so a person's performance can be interpreted by comparing it to the performance of others—that is, the test is norm-referenced (Merhrens and Lehmann, 1987, pp. 7-8).

II. Test Classification

  A. Cognitive measures: Measures of maximum performance (how well a person will do when motivated to obtain as high a score as possible).

    1. Aptitude tests: These tests are designed to predict success in some future learning activity.

    2. Achievement tests: These tests are designed to indicate the degree of success in some past learning activity.

  B. Non-cognitive measures: measures of typical behavior (procedures of this type are concerned with what the individual will do rather than what they can do).

    1. Interest inventories

    2. Personality inventories

    3. Attitude inventories

III. Test Characteristics

The following information is a list of components that are essential when determining the adequacy of any assessment (formal or informal).

  A. Reliability: Refers to the consistency and stability of assessment results.

  B. Validity: Refers to the meaningfulness and appropriateness of the uses and interpretations to be made of assessment results. Validity is the most significant aspect of any test.

  C. Normative information: A comparison can be made of one student's results to that of other students who have taken the same test. According to Linn and Gronlund (1995), there are four basic types of test norms:

  Grade norms (grade equivalents): Grade group in which student's raw score is average. Note: Grade equivalents should never be interpreted literally; at best, they are only a rough guide as to the level of test performance.

  Percentile norms (percentile ranks or percentile scores): Percentage of students in the reference group who fall below student's raw score.

  Standard-score norms (standard scores): distance of student's raw score above or below the mean of the reference group in terms of standard deviation units (p. 444).

Stanines: Stanines are essentially groups of percentile ranks, with the entire group of scores divided into nine parts, with the largest number of individuals falling in the middle stanines, and fewer students falling at the extremes. Few tests in common usage use stanines today, although these scores can be useful in understanding the relative range of a student's performance (A. Canter, 1998, p. 119).

Note: It is important that teachers always check the latest copyright date to ensure that the norms have been updated continually in an effort to keep the test current.

IV. Test Interpretation

A. Norm-referenced interpretation: Describes the performance in terms of the relative position held in some known group. Individual scores are compared to standard or group scores. A norm-referenced test is designed to provide a measure of performance that is interpretable in terms of an individual's relative standing in some known group. Example: Jane typed better than 85 percent of the class members.

B. Criterion-referenced interpretation: Describes the specific performance that was demonstrated. The criterion-referenced test is designed to provide a measure of performance that is interpretable in terms of a clearly defined and delimited domain of learning task. Example: Jane typed 40 words per minute without error.

Test Administration Checklist

The following checklist will guide the new special education teacher through his or her first test administration. The checklist is divided into three main sections. Space is provided for the teacher to add additional items to each section.

Prior to Test

_____ Send parent notification of test date and time. Request parent permission prior as directly by school system policy.

_____ Inform the student or students in advance of the upcoming test date.

_____ Thoroughly read the examiner's manual of the test to be administered.

_____ Thoroughly read the student's test booklet to ensure that there are no discrepancies between the booklet and the examiner's manual.

_____ Check and assemble all test materials. Test materials could possibly include

#2 pencils

Stop watch

Student booklets

Examiner's manual

Scratch paper

Calculators

Testing—Do Not Disturb Sign

_____ Select and reserve testing location. The test location should be comfortable and free from distractions.

_____ Review the test directions the day before testing. Highlight important notes or items in the directions. In addition, colored adhesive tabs can be placed in the examiner's manual to mark each section of the test.

_____ _____

_____ _____

_____ _____

During the Test

_____ Post the testing sign on the outside door of test location.

_____ Request students to sign in if testing in a large group.

_____ Distribute test materials to student.

_____ Read the test directions to students.

_____ Write the start time of the test in a highly visible location when testing in a large group.

_____ Monitor students.

_____ _____

_____ _____

_____ _____

After the Test

_____ Collect all test materials carefully and promptly.

_____ Collect pencils, scratch paper, or other materials given to student or students for testing purposes.

_____ Remove testing sign from door.

_____ Return to classroom and count test materials.

_____ Place order to replenish test materials.

_____ Store all tests in a secure location until they can be sent for scoring or the teacher arranges to score the test.

_____ Write formal report on test results.

_____ _____

_____ _____

_____ _____

Common Educational Assessments*

- Wechsler Intelligence Scale for Children-Revised (WISC-R)
    - Author: David Wechsler
    - Age Group: Child or Teen
    - Purpose: Assesses mental ability in children (p. 36).
- Bender Visual Motor Gestalt Test
    - Author: Lauretta Bender
    - Age Group: All ages
    - Purpose: Assess the visual-motor functions of individuals from age three years to adulthood. Also used in the evaluation of developmental problems in children, learning disabilities, retardation, psychosis, and organic brain disorders (p. 37).
- Differential Aptitude Tests Battery
    - Author: Manjula Makerjee
    - Age Group: Child and Teen
    - Purpose: Identifies specific areas of academic aptitude for students ages 11-13 (p. 365).
- House-Tree-Person Technique: Revised Manual (H-T-P)
    - Author: John N. Buck
    - Age Group: All ages
    - Purpose: Assess personality disturbances in individuals in psychotherapy, school, and research settings. May be used with the culturally disadvantaged, educationally deprived, mentally retarded, and the aged (p. 157).
- Iowa Tests of Basic Skills, Forms 7 and 8 (ITBS)
    - Author: A. N. Hieronymous, E. F. Lindquist, and H. D. Hoover
    - Age Group: Grades K-9
    - Purpose: Assesses the development of basic academic skills in students Grades K-9. Identifies individual student's strengths and weaknesses and evaluates the effectiveness of instructional programs (p. 372).
- The Minnesota Multi-Phasic Personality Inventory: The Individual Form (MMPI)
    - Author: Strake R. Hathaway and Charnley McKinley
    - Age Group: Teen and Adult
    - Purpose: Assess individual personality. Used for clinical diagnosis and research on psychopathology (p. 119).

---

*Adapted from R. C. Sweetland and D. J. Keyser, 1984

- Otis-Lennon Mental Ability Test
  - Author: Arthur S. Otis and Roger T. Lennon
  - Age Group: Grades K.5-12
  - Purpose: Assess general mental ability or scholastic aptitude (p. 387).
- Peabody Picture Vocabulary Test—Revised (PPVT—R)
  - Author: Lloyd M. Dunn and Leota M. Dunn
  - Age Group: All ages
  - Purpose: Measures hearing vocabulary for standard American English, estimates verbal ability and scholastic aptitude. Used with non-English speaking students; to screen for mental retardation or giftedness; as part of a comprehensive battery; and to screen applicants for jobs requiring good oral vocabulary (pp. 574-575).
- Rotter Incomplete Sentences Blank
  - Author: Julian B. Rotter
  - Age Group: Teen and Adult
  - Purpose: Assess personality of adolescents and adults (p. 132).
- Slosson Intelligence Test (SIT)/Slosson Oral Reading Test (SORT)
  - Author: Richard L. Slosson
  - Age Group: All ages
  - Purpose: Measures the mental age, IQ, and reading level of children and adults. Used by psychologists, guidance counselors, special educators, learning disabilities teachers, and remedial reading teachers to provide a quick assessment of a person's mental abilities (pp. 31-32).
- Stanford Measurement Series—Stanford Achievement Test: 7th Edition
  - Author: Eric F. Gardner, Herbert C. Rudman, Bjorn Karlsen, and Jack Merwin
  - Age Group: Grades 1.5-9.9
  - Purpose: Assess school achievement status of children from first through tenth grade (p. 396).
- Stanford-Binet Intelligence Scale: Form L-M
  - Author: Lewis M. Terman and Maud A. Merrill
  - Age Group: All ages
  - Purpose: Measures an individual's mental abilities. Used to substantiate questionable scores from group tests and when the subject has physical, language, or personality disorders that rule out group testing (p.33).
- Vineland Social Maturity Scale
  - Author: Edgar A. Doll
  - Age Group: All ages
  - Purpose: Measures successive stage of social competence or adaptive behavior. Used to measure normal development or individual differ-

ences that may be significant in cases of handicaps such as mental deficiencies and emotional disturbances in order to plan therapy or individual education (p. 16).

- Wide Range Achievement Test (WRAT)
  - Author: Joseph F. Jastak and Sarah Jastak
  - Age Group: Child and Teen
  - Purpose: Measures the basic educational skills of word recognition, spelling and arithmetic, and identifies individuals with learning difficulties. Used for education placement, measuring school achievement, vocational assessment, job placement, and training (p. 408).
- Test of Written Language (TOWL)
  - Author: Donald D. Hammill and Stephen C. Larsen
  - Age Group: Grades 2-12
  - Purpose: Identifies students grades 2-12 who have problem in written expression, pinpointing specific areas of deficit (p. 225).

Writing a Legal and Effective Individualized Education Program

8

The writing of an individualized education program (IEP) for a student with a disability is one of the most important and monumental tasks the new special education teacher will be required to undertake during the school year. The IEP is a legal document that is mandated by the Individuals with Disabilities Education Act 1997 (IDEA). The IEP is a plan that must be reviewed and developed at least annually by a team of individuals in order to meet the educational needs of the student with a disability. The IEP can be revised or revisited at any time. The authors recommend reviewing the plan on a regular basis throughout the year in order to chart student progress and note significant problem areas.

If the educational strategies, current placement, or any other factor in the plan appears to be ineffective, the special education teacher should organize a team meeting and make the appropriate adjustments. In addition, an IEP is developed after the student is found to be eligible for services and following a three-year reevaluation. According to the regulations, the team must be composed of a regular education teacher if the student will or possibly will be participating in an inclusive setting; a school administrator or someone who has knowledge of general curriculum, resources of outside public agencies, and qualified to supervise the implementation of the IEP; the parents of the student; and the student when deemed appropriate. Other individuals may participate as part of the IEP team at the parent's discretion. A tremendous amount of time and skill is involved in writing a plan that can both meet the legal requirements or mandates and effectively communicate the needs of the students. The plan serves as the instructional blueprint for the special and regular education teacher.

In this chapter, the authors have identified two basic skills that the special education teacher should possess before writing his or her first IEP of the school year. First, the new teacher should have a clear understanding of the IDEA '97 regulations that specifically address the content of the IEP before attempting to write his or her first. The essential information that every IEP is legally required to contain is specifically stated in Section 300.347 of the regulations. The components that comprise Section 300.347

address the following: information relating to the child's present levels of performance; how deficits will be addressed and progress measured; the need for specific special education services, related services, and supplementary aids; the extent the disabled child will not be placed with nondisabled students; testing modifications; the projected start and end dates of a child's IEP; how the student is progressing toward the annual goals; how the parents were informed; and transition services. The authors provide the teacher with a summary and reference for each component in this chapter.

Secondly, the special education teacher must possess the ability to communicate all student information accurately and succinctly in order to write an effective IEP. The teacher should utilize language that can be easily understood by most audiences, provide information that is of an objective nature, and formulate an overall plan of action that can easily be followed by special and regular education teachers, support personnel, and parents. The plan should be written on a personal level with positive overtones. In this chapter, the authors focus on the content aspect of the IEP in order to assist the new special education teacher in writing a plan that will survive a due process hearing. The chapter is structured in a format that will enlighten the teacher as to the legal aspects of the IEP and assist him or her with writing an effective plan. The authors have included additional summaries of IDEA '97 that pertain to the IEP and provide the new teacher with an *IEP Conference Summary* form at the end of the chapter.

Section 1: The Legal Requirements of an IEP—Section 300.347: Content of IEP

Present Level of Performance

1. A statement of the child's present levels of educational performance to include

    (i)   How the child's disability affects the child's involvement and progress in the general curriculum

          or

    (ii) For preschool children, as appropriate, how the disability affects the child's participation in appropriate activities *(Federal Register/No. 48*, Volume 64/Section 300.347 (a) (1) (i) (ii)/1999).

Student Annual Goals and Objectives

2. A statement of measurable annual goals, including benchmarks or short-term objectives related to

    (i)   Meeting the child's needs that result from the child's disability to enable the child to be involved in and progress in the general curriculum, or for preschool children, as appropriate, to participate in appropriate activities.

(ii) Meeting each of the child's other educational needs that result from the child's disability *(Federal Register/No. 48*, Volume 64/Section 300.347 (a) (2) (i) (ii)/1999)

Student Services, Supplementary Aids, and Program Modifications or Supports

3. A statement of the special education and related services and supplementary aids and services to be provided to the child, or on behalf of the child, and a statement of the program modifications or supports for school personnel that will be provided for the child:

   (i) To advance appropriately toward attaining the annual goals.

   (ii) To be involved and progress in the general curriculum in accordance with paragraph (a) (1) of this section and to participate in extracurricular and other nonacademic activities.

   (iii) To be educated and participate with other children with disabilities and nondisabled children in the activities described in this section *(Federal Register/No. 48*, Volume 64/Section 300.347 (a) (3) (i) (ii) (iii)/1999).

Student Placement: Academic, Extracurricular, and Nonacademic Activities

4. An explanation of the extent, if any, to which the child will not participate with nondisabled children in the regular class and in the activities described in paragraph (3) of this section *(Federal Register/No. 48*, Volume 64/Section 300.347 (a) (4)/1999).

Individual Modifications for Student Achievement Assessments

5. (i) A statement of any individual modifications in the administration of State or district-wide assessments of student achievement that are needed in order for the child to participate in the assessment.

   (ii) If the IEP team determines that the child will not participate in a particular state or district-wide assessment of student achievement (or part of an assessment), a statement of

   a. Why that assessment is not appropriate for the child

   and

   b. How the child will be assessed *(Federal Register/No. 48*, Volume 64/Section 300.347 (a) (5)(i) (ii) (A) (B)/1999).

Student Service Dates, Frequency, Location, Duration, and Program Modifications

6. The projected date for the beginning of their services and modifications described in paragraph (a) (3) of this section, and the anticipated frequency, location, and duration of those services and modifications *(Federal Register/No. 48*, Volume 64/Section 300.347 (a) (6)/1999).

Student Progress: Measuring, Evaluating, and Informing Parents

7. A statement of
   (i) How the child's progress toward the annual goals described in paragraph (a) (2) of this section is measured.
   (ii) How the child's parents will be regularly informed (through such means as periodic report cards), at least as often as parents are informed of their nondisabled children's progress, of
      a. Their child's progress toward the annual goals.
      b. The extent to which that progress is sufficient to enable the child to achieve the goals by the end of the year *(Federal Register/No. 48*, Volume 64/Section 300.347 (a) (7)(i) (ii) (A) (B)/1999).

Transition Services

The IEP must include

1. For each student with a disability beginning at age 14 (or younger if determined appropriate by the IEP team), and updated annually, a statement of the transition service needs of the student under the applicable components of the student's IEP that focuses on the student's courses of study (such as participation in advanced-placement courses or a vocational education program); and

2. For each student beginning at age 16 (or younger, if determined appropriate by the IEP team), a statement of needed transition services for the student, including, if appropriate, a statement of the interagency responsibilities or any needed linkages *(Federal Register/No. 48*, Volume 64/Section 300.347 (b) (1) (2)/1999).

Transfer of Rights

In a state that transfers rights at the age of majority, beginning at least one year before a student reaches the age of majority under state law, the student's IEP must include a statement that the student has been informed of his or her rights under Part B of the Act, if any, that will transfer to the student on reaching the age of majority, consistent with Section 300.517 (*Federal Register/No. 48*, Volume 64/Section 300.347 (b)(c)/1999).

Students with Disabilities Convicted as Adults and Incarcerated in Adult Prisons

Special rules concerning the content of IEPs for students with disabilities convicted as adults and incarcerated in adult prisons are contained in 300.31 (b) and (c) (*Federal Register/No. 48*, Volume 64/Section 300.347 (b) (d)/1999).

Section 2: Recommendations for IEP Components

Present Level of Performance

The authors view the present level of educational performance as one of the most important components of the IEP. In this section, an educational profile of the student is developed with input from the IEP team. The profile should provide the reader with a comprehensive perspective of the student and provide the framework for the other IEP components. The present level of education performance is typically written in a narrative format and can easily read by parents, students, and other professionals. The teacher is encouraged to write in non-technical language and utilize the student's first name when appropriate. This will improve the readability and personalize the document. The authors consider the information below to be crucial in order to produce the present levels of educational performance component of the IEP. The special education teacher should write specific statements that address each area listed (as appropriate):

_____ Current test/evaluation data

_____ Vision and hearing screening

_____ Student achievement

_____ Communication skills

_____ Strengths and weaknesses (academic, social, and so on)

_____ Social adaptation skills

_____ Fine and gross motor skills

_____ Psychomotor Skills

_____ Review student progress in the special education classroom

Student Annual Goals and Objectives

Annual goals are statements that address the student's areas of weakness that were identified in the present levels of performance section of the IEP.

The goals should generally state what the student will be able to do by the ending date of the IEP. For example:

- Susan will be able to complete a simple job application form.
- Susan will increase her reading comprehension skills.

An *objective* is a description of a performance you want learners to be able to exhibit before you consider them competent. An object describes an intended result of instruction, rather than a process of instruction itself (Mager, 1984, p. 5). Objectives support the annual goals and must be measurable. A good objective will specifically state what the learner is to do, under what conditions the performance will occur, and the quality level of the performance. Remember that every objective must have a review date, method of evaluation, and criteria for mastery. For example:

- Given the personal information section on a simple job application, the student will complete the section with less that five errors.
- Given a selected story in the student's basal reader, the student will read the story silently and then answer four out of five comprehension questions correctly.

Student Services, Supplementary Aids, and Program Modifications or Supports

- Special education services: State specific special education program and environment in which the student will be serviced.
- Related services areas: occupational therapy, physical therapy, adaptive PE, special and regular transportation, counseling services, and so on.
- Assistive techonolgy devices or services

Student Placement: Academic, Extracurricular, and Nonacademic Activities

- Academic: core curriculum area, exploratory, specialty, or elective classes
- Extracurricular: clubs, athletic teams, cheerleading, and so on
- Nonacademic: lunch, recess, assemblies, and so on

Individual Modifications for Student Achievement Assessments

- Special education students must be assessed during the school year.
- The IEP team must state an alternative assessment method if the student is not going to participate in the statewide testing program.
- IDEA '98 allows for reasonable test accommodations.

- Some examples of acceptable test accommodations for standardized test are as follows:

  - Small group testing

  - Individual testing

  - Read test to student

  - Provide alternative response methods

  - Test in a room with carpet

  - Provide student with a study carrel

Student Service Dates, Frequency, Location, Duration, and Program Modifications

- Specifically state the exact start and end dates of the IEP.

- The IEP should list the school or facility for location.

- Frequency and duration—"how often and for how long."

- Program modifications refer to the adaptations the teacher is implementing in order for the student be successful in the classroom.

Student Progress: Measuring, Evaluating, Informing Parents, Transition Services

- Examples of measurement and evaluation tools: Teacher-made tests, textbook unit tests, standardized test, behavior rating scale, class point system, and teacher observation.

- Informing parents: School report card, school progress report, weekly progress report, telephone parents, and parent-teacher conferences.

- A transition plan must be developed for students age 14. A good transition plan will address the student's needs, interest, and aptitudes. Transition activities can include community, daily living, and employment experiences. Transition plans should address high school programs of study and post-secondary options for older students.

Section 3: Additional Summaries of Important IEP Regulations*

Section 300.342: When IEPs Must Be In Effect

1. A student's IEP must be in effect at the beginning of the school year.

2. A student's IEP must be in effect before he/she can receive special education and related services.

---

*(As cited in *Federal Register/Vol. 64*, No. 48/Friday, March 12, 1999/Rules and Regulations)

3. A student's IEP must be implemented as soon as possible following the meeting.

Section 300.343: IEP Meetings

1. Each public agency is responsible for initiating and conducting meetings for the purpose of developing, reviewing, and revising the IEP of a child with a disability or an IFSP for each child with a disability aged 3 through 5.

2. Each public agency shall ensure that an offer of services in accordance with an IEP is made to parents within a reasonable period of time from the agency's receipt of parent consent to an initial evaluation.

3. A meeting to develop an IEP must be conducted within 30 days of determination that a child needs special education and related services.

4. The IEP team must meet and review at least annually the student's IEP and determine if goals and objectives are being achieved.

5. Revise IEP as appropriate to address:
    -   Lack of expected progress toward annual goals
    -   Results of any reevaluations
    -   Information about the child provided to, or by, the parents
    -   Child's anticipated needs
    -   Other matters

Section 300.344: IEP Team

1. Parents of child

2. At least one regular education teacher who is, or may be, responsible for implementing the IEP. If the child has more than one regular education teacher, the LEA may designate which teacher/teachers will participate in the IEP team meeting (if the child is or may be participating in the regular education environment).

3. At least one special education teacher. This should be the teacher who will be responsible for implementing the IEP.

4. A representative of the LEA who

    Is qualified to provide or supervise the provision of specifically designed instruction to meet the unique needs of children with disabilities.

    Is knowledgeable about general curriculum.

    Is knowledgeable about the availability of resources.

5. An individual who can interpret the instructional implications of evaluation results.

6. At the discretion of the parent or the agency, other individuals who have knowledge or special expertise regarding the child, including related service personnel as appropriate.

7. If appropriate, the child. (Note: The public agency shall invite a student with a disability of any age if a purpose of the meeting will be the consideration of the statement of transition services needs or statement of needed transition services for the student.)

8. Transition services participants.

   The public agency shall invite a representative of any other agency that is likely to be responsible for providing or paying for transition services.

Section 300.345: Parent Participation

1. Each public agency shall take steps to ensure that one or both of the parents of a child with a disability are present at each IEP meeting or are afforded the opportunity to participate, including

   Notifying parents of meeting early enough to ensure that they will attend.

   Schedule meeting at a mutually agreed upon time and place.

2. Notice must include purpose, time, and location of meeting and who will be in attendance.

3. If neither parent can attend, the public agency shall use other methods to ensure parent participation, including individual or conference telephone calls.

4. A meeting may be conducted without a parent in attendance if the public agency is unable to convince the parents that they should attend:

   Detailed records of telephone calls made or attempted and the results of these calls.

   Copies of correspondence sent to parents and response received.

   Detailed records of visits made to parent's home or place of employment and the results.

5. The public agency shall take whatever action is necessary to ensure that the parents understand the proceedings at a meeting, including arranging for an interpreter for parents with deafness or whose native language is other than English.

6. The public agency shall give the parent, or request, a copy of the IEP. (Note: It is also important that the special education teacher give the parents a copy of their legal rights and document the action.)

Essential Information for the Individualized Education Program Conference

Note: The following information must be collected and reviewed by the special education teacher prior to the individualized education program conference.

_____ Review current levels of performance:

    1. Educational assessments

        a. Intelligence

        b. Academic achievement

        c. Learning style

        d. Adaptive behavior

        e. Social/emotional

        f. Fine and gross motor

    2. Audiological assessment

    3. Speech/language pathologist assessment

    4. Physical therapy assessment

    5. Occupational therapy assessment

    6. Fine and gross motor skills assessment

    7. Current medical status

_____ Review current individualized education program:

    1. Goals and objectives (Annotate the mastered goals and objectives on current IEP)

    2. Related services: transportation, physical therapy, occupational therapy, speech and language therapy, other

    3. Student's current placement:

        _____ Regular class   _____ Resource class

        _____ Separate/self-contained class

        _____ Public separate school Facility

        _____ Private separate school facility

        _____ Public residential facility   _____ Private residential facility

        _____ Homebound/hospital environment

    4. Student's discipline plan

    5. Student's behavior management plan

    6. Student's standardized testing modifications

    7. Student's transition plan

_____ Review student's performance in regular education classes

_____ Test grades   _____ Quiz grades   _____ Homework completion

_____ Class participation   _____ On-task behavior   _____ Conduct

_____ Review general student information:

1. Attendance record

2. Discipline record

3. School transcript (high school students only)

4. Student program of study (high school students only)

Transition and the Special Education Student

Transitions occur naturally throughout our life span as we move through major life changes. For most of us, we "transition" at approximately age five or six to public school, exit school at approximately age eighteen to post-school life options of work, marriage, college, or the military, and many of us retire at approximately age sixty-two. All of these transitions involve a certain amount of stress; students with disabilities may have greater adjustment problems during their life transitions due to fewer background experiences, lower self-esteem, or fewer social/coping skills. There are certain things special education teachers can do to facilitate transitions for their students.

All students with IEPs must have Individual Transition Plans by the age of 14 or the end of the eighth grade. The content of the ITP must address post-school desires and needs of the student. It must be reviewed annually and the present level of performance, the goals, and the objectives should be focused on post-school outcomes. The student and any community agency personnel involved in transition planning, such as a vocational rehabilitation counselor, must be involved in the annual ITP meeting. Some school districts develop ITPs separately from the IEPs. Others incorporate the transition plan into the student's IEP. Teachers should contact their local school district for specific guidelines.

Existing requirements were expanded in IDEA '97 for the IEP to include transition service needs (beginning at age 14 and updated annually) that focus on his/her courses of study. This should include, when appropriate, the interagency responsibilities or needed linkages (beginning at age 16 or younger) and a statement that the child has been informed of the rights that will transfer to him/her on reaching the age of majority (*CEC Today*, 1999). For example, students planning to attend college should be informed of their rights to modifications in college or technical school classrooms under the Americans with Disabilities Act (ADA) (Public Law 101-336).

Transition may be defined as "the process of planning for changes throughout a student's life after high school; however, planning for changes throughout life is a more accurate definition" (Mastropieri and Scruggs, 2000). Wehman (1996) has found that planning for transitions at all ages promotes social and emotional well-being of students with disabilities. As special education teachers, you will be responsible for planning the transitions that will occur for your students.

Planning major life transitions such as enrollment in full-day public school and the change from school to post-school is mandated by IDEA. However, any change in a student's schedule, placement, school, or even transportation should be viewed as an opportunity to help the student prepare for a change. For example, a child moving from a half-day preschool program to full-day first grade might need to prepare for navigating the lunchroom, playground, library, or other new physical environments as well as classroom skills such as sitting in a desk, raising your hand to be called on, following instructions, taking turns, walking down the hall in line, and so on.

Changing schools can be a very traumatic event for students with disabilities. Going from elementary to middle school or middle school to high school both involve several adjustments. A primer or simple booklet providing useful information for students and parents given out well in advance of the change can be very helpful. Another helpful idea is for the student to actually go over and visit the next environment so he/she will be familiar with the physical layout of the new building. A teacher-made transition guide is fairly simple to make. Be sure to keep in mind the reading level of the student for whom the book is being created. Booklets for students making the transition from middle school to high school could include school calendar, bell schedule, absence policy, dress code, code of conduct, extra curricular activities, and graduation options. If grade-level changes are made smoothly, there is a greater likelihood that the post-school transition will go well due to positive experiences with change in the past.

In conclusion, preparing for post-school outcomes should be an exciting time for adolescents. It is the role of the teacher to explore the possibilities for post-school options with each student. Realistic goals need to be set keeping each student's strengths, weaknesses, interests, and abilities in mind. The transition planning process provides an excellent opportunity to increase the self-advocacy and self-determination skills for students as they prepare for adulthood. Many students with disabilities have traditionally not been afforded the same number of opportunities to make decisions and choices as students without disabilities. Empowering students with disabilities to be self-directed should be the ultimate goal of the special education teacher, and working with the student on transition planning can help to empower the student. Remember, the more advanced preparation, the better!

Professional Development and the Special Education Teacher

Professional development can be defined as any course of action taken by a teacher for the purpose of increasing his or her knowledge in a particular educational field or area of expertise. Professional development is essential in order for both new and veteran special education teachers to keep pace with the advancements in teaching methodologies, practices, and instructional materials. In addition, the field of special education has been affected by advancements in technology. Teachers should have adequate computer skills and be able to integrate technology into their classrooms. Special education teachers have the additional professional responsibility of keeping abreast of new legal developments in the field that could have an impact on students with disabilities or special education programs.

In this chapter, the authors suggest three main ways in which the new teacher can stay current in his or her field or area. First, the authors recommend that the new special education teacher join at least one professional education organization. Often these organizations supply their members with valuable information in the form of journals or newsletters, hold annual conferences, offer members liability coverage, and provide the new teacher with networking opportunities. Next, new teachers can read educational journals and books in the profession of special education on a regular basis. The media centers of most schools have educational journals and books available for staff members. However, if the new teacher finds his or her school's media center lacking in a particular area, check with the head librarian to see if additional resources can be ordered. Finally, the new teacher can enroll in advanced college courses or staff development classes offered through his or her school system. Typically, staff development classes are offered at low or no cost to the teacher, scheduled after school hours or during the summer, and give credit toward recertification.

The authors recommend that the new special education teacher begin developing a professional development plan as soon as the school year is underway. The plan should include short and long-range professional goals, a timeline for goal completion, and note the new teacher's particular areas of interest. In this chapter, the authors provide information that will assist the new teacher in formulating his or her professional development plan. The reader will find a professional development plan form and listings of education organizations, journals, and reference books in the pages that follow. The new special education teacher must remember that professional development is a continuous process and an individual responsibility.

Form 10.1 Professional development plan

School Year:_____

Teacher:_____

Certification Number: _____Expiration Date:_____

Certification Area/Areas: List

_____

_____

Short-Range Professional Goals (completion within one year):

Professional Goal	Completion Date
1.	
2.	
3.	
4.	

Short-Range Professional Goals (completion within five year):

Professional Goal	Completion Date
1.	
2.	
3.	
4.	

Professional Organizations for the Special Education Teacher

American Federation of Teachers (AFT)
   555 New Jersey Ave NW, 10th Floor
   Washington, DC 20001
   Telephone: (202) 879-4400

Council for Children with Behavioral Disorders (CCBD)
   c/o The Council for Exceptional Children
   1920 Association Drive
   Reston, VA 20192-1589
   William Evans, President
   Telephone: (703) 620-3660
   Fax: (703) 264-9494

Council for Exceptional Children (CEC)
   1920 Association Drive
   Reston, VA 22091-1587
   Nancy D. Safer, Contact
   Telephone: (703) 620-3660 or (703) 264-9462
   Fax: (703) 264-9494

Division on Career Development and Transition (DCDT)
   c/o The Council for Exceptional Children
   1920 Association Drive
   Reston, VA 20191
   Robert Miller, President
   Telephone: (703) 620-3660
   Fax: (703) 264-9494

Division for Early Childhood (DEC)
   Council for Exceptional Children
   1920 Association Drive
   Reston, VA 20191-1589
   Tess Bennett, President
   Telephone: (703) 620-3660
   Fax: (703) 264-9494

Division for Learning Disabilities
   c/o Council for Exceptional Children
   1920 Association Drive
   Reston, VA 20191-1589
   Web site: **www.dldcec.org**

American Association on Mental Retardation
   Web site: **www.aamr.org**

Division on Visual Impairment (DVI)
c/o Council for Exceptional Children
1920 Association Drive
Reston, VA 20191-1589
Roseanna Davidson, President
Telephone: (703) 620-3660
Fax: (703) 264-9494

Foundation for Exceptional Children (FEC)
1920 Association Drive
Reston, VA 20191
Ken Collins, Executive Director
Telephone: (703) 620-1054
Fax: (703) 264-9494

National Alliance of Black School Educators (NABSE)
2816 Georgia Avenue NW
Washington, D©20001
Quentin Lawson, Executive Director
Telephone: (202) 483-1549
Fax: (202) 483-8323

National Association of Professional Educators (NAPE)
412 1st Street SE
Washington, D©20003
Philip Strittmatter, Executive Secretary
Telephone: (202) 484-8969
Fax: (202) 863-9361

National Association of Early Childhood Teacher Educators (NAFCTE)
c/o Dr. Jean Isenberg
9671 Mason Bluff Ct.
Burke, VA 22015-3148
Dr. Jean Isenberg, President
Telephone: (703) 993-2037
Fax: (703) 993-2013

National Education Association (NEA)
1201 16th Street, NW
Washington, DC 20036
Telephone: (202) 833-4000

Web Sites

The Council for Exceptional Children: **www.cec.sped.org**

Council for Children with Behavior Disorders: **www.ccbd.net**

Division for Learning Disabilities: **www.dldcec.org**

Division of Early Childhood: **www.dec-sped.org/**

American Association on Mental Retardation: **www.aamr.org**

Council for Learning Disabilities: **http://coe.winthrop.edu/cld/**

Adaptive Environments Universal Designs: **www.adaptenv.org/**

Professional Periodicals for the Special Education Teacher

The ADHD Report
Attention Deficit Hyperactivity Disorders Report
Guilford Publications Inc.
72 Spring Street
New York, NY 10012
Telephone: (212) 431-9800
Toll-free: (800) 365-7006
Fax: (212) 966-6708
Publishing schedule: Six times a year
Cost: $93.00

Advances in Learning and Behavioral Disabilities
JAJ Press Inc.
55 Old Post Road
Suite 2
PO Box 1678
Greenwich, CT 06836-1678
Telephone: (203) 661-7602
Fax: (203) 661-0792
Publishing schedule: Irregular
Cost: $73.25

The American Journal of Occupational Therapy
American Occupational Therapy Association
4720 Montgomery Lane
Rockville, MD 20824
Telephone: (301) 652-2682
Fax: (301) 652-7711
Publishing schedule: Ten times a year
Cost: $120.00

Behavioral Disorders
Council for Exceptional Children
1920 Association Drive
Reston, VA 20191
Telephone: (703) 620-3660
Toll-free: (800) 232-7323
Publishing schedule: Four times a year
Cost: $50.00

Beyond Behavior
    Council for Exceptional Children
    1920 Association Drive
    Reston, VA 20191
    Telephone: (703) 620-3660
    Toll-free: (800) 232-7323
    Fax: (703) 264-9494
    Publishing schedule: Three times a year
    Cost: $35.00

Campus Opportunities for Students with Learning Differences
    Octameron Associates
    Box 2748
    Alexandria, VA 22301
    Telephone: (703) 836-5480
    Fax: (703) 836-5650
    Publishing schedule: Unknown
    Cost: $4.00

Career Development for Exceptional Individuals
    Council for Exceptional Children
    1920 Association Drive
    Reston, VA 20191
    Telephone: (703) 620-3660
    Toll-free: (800) 232-7323
    Fax: (703) 264-9494
    Publishing schedule: Two times a year
    Cost: $20.00

Directions: Technology in Special Education
    DREAMMS for Kinds, Inc.
    763 Tasha Drive
    Clearwater, FL 34621-1223
    Telephone: (813) 781-7711
    Fax: (813)781-7711
    Publishing schedule: Twelve times a year
    Cost: Unknown

The Directory For Exceptional Children
    Porter Sargent Publishers Inc.
    11 Beacon Street
    Suite 1400
    Boston, MA 02108
    Telephone: (617) 523-1021
    Publishing schedule: Irregular (Every two to three years)
    Cost: $60.00

Directory of Facilities and Services for Learning Disabilities
Academic Therapy Publications
20 Commercial Boulevard
Novato, CA 94949-6191
Telephone: (415) 883-3314
Fax: (415) 883-3720
Publishing schedule: One time a year
Cost: $4.00

Early Childhood Reporter: Children with Special Needs and Their Families
LRP Publications
747 Dresher Road
Suite 500
Horsham, PA 19044
Telephone: (215) 784-0860
Toll-free: (800) 341-7874
Publishing schedule: Twelve times a year
Cost: $155.00

Educating At-Risk Youth
National Professional Resources
PO Box 1479
25 South Regent Street
Port Chester, NY 10573
Telephone: (914) 937-8879
Fax: (914) 937-9327
Publishing schedule: Ten times a year
Cost: $68.00 one-year/$99.00 two-year

Educating Exceptional Children
Dushkin Publishing Group, Inc.
Sluice Dock
Guiford, CT 06437
Telephone: (203) 453-4351
Toll-free: (800) 338-5578
Publishing schedule: One time a year
Cost: $12.95

Exceptional Children
Council for Exceptional Children
1920 Association Drive
Reston, VA 20191
Telephone: (703) 620-2660
Toll-free: 800-232-7323
Fax: (703) 264-9494
Publishing schedule: Four times a year
Cost: $58.00

Focus on Exceptional Children
  Love Publishing Company
  1777 South Bellaire Street
  Denver, CO 80222
  Telephone: (303) 757-2579
  Fax: (303) 782-5683
  Publishing Schedule: Nine times a year
  Cost: $40.00

Focus on Learning Problems in Mathematics
  Center for Teaching and Learning Mathematics
  PO Box 3149
  Framingham, MA 01701
  Telephone: (508) 877-7895
  Fax: (508) 788-3600
  Publishing schedule: Four times a year
  Cost: $30.00 (individuals)

Intervention in School and Clinic
  Pro-Ed Inc.
  8700 Shoal Creek Boulevard
  Austin, TX 78757
  Telephone: (512) 451-3246
  Fax: (512) 451-8542
  Publishing schedule: Five times a year
  Cost: $35.00 (Individuals)

The Journal for Vocational Special Needs
  National Association of Vocational Education Special Needs Personnel
  6100 154th Avenue North
  Clearwater, FL 34620
  Telephone: (813) 531-3531
  Fax: (813) 536-9109
  Publishing schedule: Three times a year
  Cost: $24.00

Journal of Children's Communication Development
  Council for Exceptional Children
  1920 Association Drive
  Reston, VA 20191
  Telephone: (703) 620-3660
  Fax: (703) 264-9494
  Publishing schedule: Two times a year
  Cost: $16.00

Journal of Learning Disabilities
    Pro-Ed Inc.
    8700 Shoal Creek Boulevard
    Austin, TX 78757
    Telephone: (512) 451-3246
    Fax: (512) 451-8542
    Publishing schedule: Six times a year
    Cost: $130.00

The Journal of the Association for Persons with Severe Handicaps
    Association for Person with Severe Handicaps
    29 West Susquehanna Avenue
    Baltimore, MD 21204
    Telephone: (410) 828-8274
    Fax: (410) 828-6706
    Publishing schedule: Four times a year
    Cost: Unknown

*Learning Disabilities Research and Practice: A Publication of the Division
    for Learning Disabilities, Council for Exceptional Children*
    Lawrence Eribaum Associates, Inc.
    10 Industrial Avenue
    Mahwah, NJ 07430
    Telephone: (201) 236-9500
    Fax: (201) 636-0072
    Publishing schedule: Four times a year
    Cost: $200.00

Learning Disability Quarterly
    Council for Learning Disabilities
    PO Box 40303
    Overland Park, KS 66204
    Telephone: (913) 492-2546
    Fax: (913) 492-2546
    Publishing schedule: Four times a year
    Cost: $55.00

Math Notebook
    Center for Teaching and Learning Mathematics
    PO Box 3149
    Framingham, MA 01701
    Telephone: (508) 877-7895
    Fax: (508) 788-3600
    Publishing schedule: Five times a year
    Cost: $18.00 (individuals)

Mental Retardation (Washington)
    American Association on Mental Retardation
    444 North Capitol Street Northwest
    Suite 846
    Washington, D©20001
    Telephone: (202) 387-1968
    Toll-free: (800) 424-3688
    Fax: (202) 387-2193
    Publishing schedule: Six times a year
    Cost: $95.00

Occupational Therapy in Health Care
    The Haworth Press Inc.
    10 Alice Street
    Binghamton, NY 13904
    Telephone: (607) 722-2493
    Toll-free: (800) 342-9678
    Fax: (607) 722-1424
    Publishing schedule: Four times a year
    Cost: $125.00

Preventing School Failure
    Heldref Publications
    1319 Eighteenth St. Northwest
    Washington, DC 20036
    Telephone: (202) 296-6267
    Toll-free: (800) 365-9753
    Fax: (202) 296-5149
    Publishing schedule: Four times a year
    Cost: $72.00

Remedial and Special Education
    Pro-Ed Inc.
    8700 Shoal Creek Boulevard
    Austin, TX 78757
    Telephone: (512) 451-3246
    Fax: (512) 451-8542
    Publishing schedule: Six times a year
    Cost: $120.00

Teaching Exceptional Children
    Council for Exceptional Children
    1920 Association Drive
    Reston, VA 20191
    Telephone: (703) 620-3660
    Fax: (703) 264-9494
    Publishing schedule: Six times a year
    Cost: $58.00

Reference Books for the Special Education Teacher

Accessing the General Curriculum: Making Schools Work for Students With Disabilities
Author: Nolet/McLaughlin.
Publisher: Corwin Press, Inc.
Date: 2000

An Introduction to Early Childhood Special Education
Author: Linda Dunlap
Publisher: Allyn and Bacon, Incorporated
Date: 1997

At the Crossroads: Special Educational Needs and Teacher Education
Author: John Davies and Philip Garner
Publisher: Taylor and Francis, Incorporated
Date: 7/97

Adapting Curriculum and Instruction for Special Needs Students
Author: June Bigge
Publisher: Brooks/Cole Publishing Company
Date: 2/99

Asperger Syndrome: A Practical Guide for Teachers
Author: Val Cumine
Publisher: Taylor and Francis, Incorporated
Date: 4/98

Assessing Special Needs Students
Author: Libby Cohen
Publisher: Addison Wesley Longman
Date: 1/98

Assessing Young Children with Special Needs
Authors: Benner and Belmont
Publisher: Wadsworth Publishing Company
Date: 1/98

Buzzards to Bluebirds: Improve Your Child's Learning and Behavior in 6 Weeks—Help Stop Dyslexia, School Dropouts, and School Failures
Authors: Allen Crane and Virginia Crane
Publisher: Optometric Extension Program Foundation
Date: 11/97

Cases in Special Education
Authors: Joseph Boyle and Scot Danforth
Publisher: WCB/McGraw-Hill
Date: 1/97

Change in Special Education Provision
 Authors: Richard Stakes and Garry Hornby
 Publisher: Cassell Academic
 Date: 7/97

Children with Special Needs: Assessment, Law and Practice—
 Caught in the Acts
 Author: John Friel
 Publisher: Taylor and Francis, Incorporated
 Date: 5/97

Collaboration
 Author: Sharon Cramer
 Publisher: Prentice Hall
 Date: 6/97

Collaboration: A Success Strategy for Special Educators
 Author: Sharon F. Cramer
 Publisher: Allyn and Bacon, Incorporated
 Date: 1998

Collaborative Elementary Teaching: A Casebook for Elementary Special and
 General Educators
 Author: Kathleen C. Harris
 Publisher: PRO-ED
 Date: 2/98

Collaborative Secondary Teaching: A Casebook for Secondary and
 Special Educators
 Authors: Kathleen Harris and Marcia Smith
 Publisher: PRO-ED
 Date: 2/98

Complete IEP Guide: How to Advocate for Your Special Education Child
 Author: Lawrence Siegel
 Publisher: Nolo Press
 Date: 1/98

Conducting Individualized Education Program Meetings That Withstand
 Due Process: The Informal Evidentiary Proceeding
 Author: James N. Hollis
 Publisher: Charles C. Thomas Publisher, Limited
 Date: 4/98

Controversial Issues in Special Education
 Authors: Garry Hornby and Mary Atkinson
 Publisher: Taylor and Francis, Incorporated
 Date: 6/97

Cooperative Learning and Strategies for Inclusions: Celebrating Diversity in the Classroom
    Author: Joanne Putnam
    Publisher: Paul H. Brookes Publishing Company
    Date: 6/98

Dictionary of Special Education and Rehabilitation
    Authors: Glenn Vergason and M. L. Anderegg
    Publisher: Love Publishing Company
    Date: 1/97

Drama for People with Special Needs
    Author: Ann Cattanach
    Publisher: Quite Specific Media Group, Limited
    Date: 3/97

Encounters with Autistic States: A Memorial Tribute to Frances Tustin
    Authors: Theodore Mitrani and Judith Mitrani
    Publisher: Jason Aronson Publishers
    Date: 7/97

Ending Discrimination in Special Education
    Author: Herbert Grossman
    Publisher: Charles C. Thomas Publisher, Limited
    Date: Unknown

Exceptional Learners: Introduction to Special Education
    Author: Daniel Hallahan
    Publisher: Allyn and Bacon, Incorporated
    Date: 1997

Exceptional Lives: Special Education in Today's Schools
    Author: Ann P. Turnbull
    Publisher: Prentice Hall
    Date: 7/98

Excellence for All Children Meeting Special Educational Needs
    Author: Lanham
    Publisher: Bernan Associates
    Date: 1997

Federal Outlook for Exceptional Children: Fiscal Year 1998 Budget Considerations and CEC Recommendations
    Authors: Council for Exceptional Children Staff
    Publisher: Council for Exceptional Children
    Date: 6/97

Finding Help When Your Child is Struggling in School
    Author: Lawrence Greene
    Publisher: Golden Books Adult Publishing Group
    Date: 9/98

Florida Teacher Certification Exam Emotionally Handicapped
   Author: Kathy Schnirman
   Publisher: ASAP Abstracts Publishing, Incorporated
   Date: 1/98

Foundations of Special Education: Basic Knowledge Informing Research
      and Practice
   Author: James Paul
   Publisher: Brooks/Cole Publishing Company
   Date: 1/97

Functional Curriculum for Elementary, Middle, and Secondary Age Students
      with Special Needs
   Author: Paul Wehman
   Publisher: PRO-ED
   Date: 5/97

Fundamentals of Special Education: What Every Teacher Needs to Know
   Authors: Richard Culatta and James Tompkins
   Publisher: Macmillan Library
   Date: 8/98

Good Practice in Caring for Young Children with Special Needs
   Authors: Angela Dare and Margaret O'Donovan
   Publisher: Trans-Atlantic Publications, Inc.
   Date: 9/97

Group Activities to Include Students With Special Needs: Developing
      Social Interactive Skills (2000).
   Corwin Press, Inc.

Handbook for Pre-School SEN Provision: The Code of Practice in Relation to
      the Early Years
   Author: Chris Spencer
   Publisher: Taylor and Francis, Incorporated
   Date: 4/98

Home Schooling Children with Special Needs
   Author: Sharon Hensley
   Publisher: Noble Publishing Associates
   Date: 9/97

Improving Test Perfomance of Students With Disabilities...
      On District and State Assessments (2000).
   Author: Elliott/Thurow.
   Publisher: Corwin Press, Inc.
   Date: Unknown

Including Families of Children with Special Needs. A How-To-Do-It
   Authors: Sandra Feinberg, Kathleen Deerr, Barbara Jordan and
   Michelle Langa
   Publisher: Neal-Schuman Publishers
   Date: 12/98

Including Students with Special Needs: A Practical Guide for Classroom Teachers
 Authors: Marilyn Friend and William Bursuck
 Publisher: Allyn and Bacon, Incorporated
 Date: 6/98

Inclusion: Schools for All Students
 Author: J. David Smith
 Publisher: Wadsworth Publishing Company
 Date: 12/97

Introduction to Special Education
 Author: Deborah Smith
 Publisher: Prentice Hall
 Date: 7/97

Introduction to Special Education
 Authors: Smith and Luckasson
 Publisher: Prentice Hall
 Date: 9/97

Introduction to Special Education
 Author: Wood
 Publisher: Harcourt Brace College Publishers
 Date: 4/97

Introduction to Special Education: Teaching in an Age of Challenge
 Author: Deborah Smith
 Publisher: Allyn and Bacon, Incorporated
 Date: 1998

Issues, Practices, and Concerns in Special Education
 Authors: Anthony Rotatori, J. O. Schwenn, and S. A. Burkhardt
 Publisher: Jai Press, Inc.
 Date: 9/97

Just Kids: Visiting a Class for Children with Special Needs
 Author: Ellen Senisi
 Publisher: Dutton Children's Book
 Date: 2/98

Law and Special Education
 Author: Mitchell Yell
 Publisher: Prentice Hall
 Date: 11/97

Life-Centered Career Education: A Competency-Based Approach
 Author: Donn Brolin
 Publisher: Council for Exceptional Children Staff
 Date: 1/97

Life-Centered Career Education: Modified Curriculum for Individuals with Moderate Disabilities
    Author: Robert Loyd and Donn Brolin
    Publisher: Council for Exceptional Children
    Date: 2/97

Meeting the Needs of Students of ALL Abilities: How Leaders Go Beyond Inclusion (2000).
    Author: Capper/Frattural/Keyes.
    Publisher: Corwin press, Inc.
    Date: Unknown

Modifying Standard Curriculum for High-Ability Learners
    Author: Lois F. Roets
    Publisher: Leadership Publisher, Inc.
    Date: 1/97

Multiple Voices for Ethnically Diverse Exceptional Learners
    Author: Bridgie A. Ford
    Publisher: Council for Exceptional Children
    Date: 7/97

Negotiating the Special Education Maze: A Guide for Parents and Teachers
    Authors: Winifred Anderson, Stephen Chitwood, and Deidre Hayden
    Publisher: Woodbine House
    Date: 4/97

Ordinary Parents, Exceptional Children
    Author: Robert A. Naseef
    Publisher: Carol Publishing Group
    Date: 2/97

Outcomes Evaluation in Children's Services: A Guide for Mental Health, Child Welfare, Juvenile Justice, and Special Education Specialists
    Author: Anne M. Christner
    Publisher: Manisse Communications Group, Incorporated
    Date: 12/97

PRAXIS II Subject Area Assessment Emotionally Handicapped
    Author: Kathy Schnirrnan
    Publisher: ASAP Abstracts Publishing, Incorporated
    Date: 1/98

PRAXIS II Subject Area Assessment Special Education
    Author: Roberta Ramsey
    Publisher: ASAP Abstracts Publisher, Incorporated
    Date: 1/98

Parent-Teacher Partnership: Practical Approaches to Meet Special Educational Needs
    Authors: Mike Blamires, Chris Robertson, and Joannan Blamires
    Publisher: Taylor and Francis, Incorporated
    Date: 8/97

Promoting Learning for Culturally and Linguistically Diverse Students:
    Classroom Applications from Contemporary Research
    Authors: Gersten Russell and Robert Jimenez
    Publisher: Brooks/Cole Publishing Company
    Date: 12/97

Public (K-12) Education's Hot Jalapenos: Topics Picantes in Special
    Education
    Authors: Carlos Bonilla and Joyce Goss
    Publisher: ICA Publishing Company
    Date: 1/97

Reading for Meaning: An Illustrated Alternative Approach to Reading
    Author: Jon Eisenson
    Publisher: PRO-ED
    Date: 7/98

Reducing Disproportionate Representation of Culturally Diverse Students in
    Special and Gifted Education
    Authors: Alfredo J. Artiles and Grace Duran
    Publisher: Council for Exceptional Children
    Date: 7/97

Serving Exceptional Students: How School Leaders Create
    Unified Systems
    Burrello/Lashley/Beatty.
    Publisher: Corwin Press, Inc.
    Date: 2000

Special Education: Common Questions—Common-Sense Answers
    Author: Thomas C. Lovitt
    Publisher: Sopris West
    Date: 1997

Special Education Desk Reference
    Authors: Mary Buchanan and Carol Weller
    Publisher: Singular Publishing Group, Incorporated
    Date: 9/93

Special Education Dictionary
    Author: LRP Publications (Firm) Staff
    Publisher: LRP Publications
    Date: 3/97

Special Education's Failed System: A Question of Eligibility
    Author: Joel Macht
    Publisher: Greenwood Publishing Group, Incorporated
    Date: 9/98

Special Education for the 21st Century
Author: Sands and Kozleski
Publisher: Brooks/Cole Publishing Company
Date: 7/99

Special Education Law in America
Author: Reed Martin
Publisher: Future Horizons, Inc.
Date: 2/97

Special Educational Needs in the Early Years
Author: Ruth A. Wilson
Publisher: Routledge
Date: 6/98

Special Education Practice: Applying the Knowledge, Affirming the Values
Author: James Paul
Publisher: Brooks/Cole Publishing Company
Date: 1/97

Special Needs Provision: Rethinking Special Needs Education
Author: Geoff Sewell
Publisher: Cassell Academic
Date: 3/97

Strategies for Communicating with Parents and Families of Exceptional Children
Authors: Roger Kroth and Denzil Edge
Publisher: Love Publishing Company
Date: 3/97

Strategies. Modifying Regular Curriculum
Author: Piazza
Publisher: Delmar Publishers
Date: 11/97

Strategies for Struggling Learners: A Guide for the Teaching Parent
Authors: Joe Sutton and Connie Sutton
Publisher: Exceptional Diagnostics
Date: 7/97

Supervising Paraeducators in School Settings. A Team Approach
Authors: Anna Pickeft and Kent Gerlach
Publisher: PRO-ED
Date: 5/97

Student Teacher to Master Teacher: A Guide for Preservice and Beginning Teachers of Students with Mild to Moderate Disabilities
Authors: Michael Rosenberg, Lawrence O'Shea, and Dorothy O'Shea
Publisher: Prentice Hall
Date: 8/97

Teaching and Advocacy
  Authors: Denny Taylor and Deborah Coughlin
  Publisher: Stenhouse Publishers
  Date: 1/97

Teaching Students with Language and Communication Disabilities
  Author: S. Jay Kuder
  Publisher: Allyn and Bacon, Incorporated
  Date: 1997

Teaching Students with Special Needs in Inclusive Settings:
    Examination Copy
  Authors: Tom E. Smith, Edward Polloway, James Patton, and
    Carol Dowdy
  Publisher: Allyn and Bacon, Incorporated
  Date: 1998

Teaching Students with Special Needs in Inclusive Settings
  Authors: Tom E. Smith and Edward A. Polloway
  Publisher: Allyn and Bacon Computer Books
  Date: 7/97 *The Special Education Teacher's Book of Lists*
  Author: Roger Pierangelo
  Publisher: The Center for Applied Research in Education
  Date: 1997

Teaching Study Skills and Strategies to Students Who Are LD, ADD and
    At-Risk
  Authors: Stephen Strichart, Charles Mangrum, and Patricia Iannuzzi
  Publisher: Allyn and Bacon, Incorporated
  Date: 4/98

Technology, Curriculum, and Professional Development: Adapting Schools
    to Meet the Needs of Students Disabilities
  Author: Cuban, Woodward (eds.).
  Publisher: Corwin Press, Inc.
  Date: 2001

Testing Students With Disabilities: Practical Strategies for Complying With
    District and State Requirements
  Author: Thurlow/Elliott/Ysseldyke.
  Publisher: Corwin Press, Inc.
  Date: 1998

The Exceptional Child in the Regular Classroom: An Educator's Guide
  Author: Lee Nielsen
  Publisher: Corwin Press, Incorporated
  Date: 1997

Theorising Special Education
  Authors: Catherine Clark, Alan Dyson, and Aan Millward
  Publisher: Routledge
  Date: 6/98

The Power of Imagery: Watch Learning Problems Disappear
  Author: Mildred Gifford
  Publisher: GiffOdess Books
  Date: 1/98

The Special Education Teacher's Book of Lists
  Author: Roger Pierangelo
  Publisher: The Center for Applied Research in Education
  Date: 1997

*The Special-Needs Reading List: An Annotated Guide to the Best
    Publications for Parents and Professionals*
  Author: Wilma K. Sweeney
  Publisher: Woodbine House
  Date: 1/98

Three Rs for Special Education
  Author: Grace Hanlon
  Publisher: Edvantage Media
  Date: 6/97

*The Whole-School Audit: Development Planning for Primary and Special
    Schools*
  Author: Brian Drakeford
  Publisher: Taylor and Francis, Incorporated
  Date: 8/97

Values into Practice in Special Education
  Author: David Thompson
  Publisher: Taylor and Francis, Incorporated
  Date: 12/97

*What Reading Research Tells Us About Children with Diverse Learning
    Needs: Bases and Basics*
  Authors: Deborah C. Simmons and E. J. Kameenui
  Publisher: Lawrence Erlbaum Associates, Incorporated
  Date: 6/98

Writing Time: Writing Strategies That Achieve Results
  Author: H. Jean Azemove
  Publisher: Harriet Jean Azemove
  Date: 1/98

Young Children with Special Needs
  Authors: Warren Umansky and Stephen R. Hooper
  Publisher: Prentice Hall
  Date: 10/97

Young Children with Special Needs: A Developmentally Appropriate Approach, Instructor's
Manual and Test Bank
Authors: Michael D. Davis, Jennifer L. Kilgo, and Michael Gamel-McCormick
Publisher: Allyn and Bacon, Incorporated
Date: 1998

Appendices

Medical Emergencies in the School Setting

Medical Emergencies in the Special Classroom

The majority of new special education teachers will enter into their first teaching positions with the skills necessary to meet the academic needs of their students and respond appropriately to various educational situations. However, a spectrum of non-educational situations that may arise requires the new teacher to react immediately and with extreme decisiveness. The most common of these situations is when a student becomes ill or injured during the school day. Numerous medical emergencies can occur to students inside and outside of the classroom. The classroom teacher is usually the first adult to respond to injured or ill students and must be able to assess their physical condition at the scene and determine the proper course of action without hesitation.

The information contained is this appendix includes a comprehensive list and description of common medical situations or emergencies that the authors have found occur most frequently in the school environment and the appropriate first aid response by the teacher. In addition, a recommended list of first aid supplies for the classroom is provided in this section. The authors utilized the *National Safety Council First Aid and CPR* (1992) book in order to obtain all medical information. The authors recommend that the new teacher take the following actions before the new school begins:

- Review the school system's policies and procedures that specifically address how teachers are to handle medical emergencies in the school environment.

- Request updated medical information from parents at the beginning of each school year. A medical history form (Form A.1) has been included in this section. The teacher should review the form and note all significant medical problems.

- The teacher should develop an emergency medical plan for all students who have a significant medical problem or condition (for example, seizures, allergic to bee stings, asthma) (Form A.2). A copy of the plan should be kept in the school's main office.

- The teacher should complete a report after each medical incident (Form A.3).

- The teacher should inform all school personnel that will have a significant amount of contact with the student of his or her medical condition or problem (for example, inform the physical education teacher if the student has asthma).

- The teacher must remember to keep a log of all medical incidents that occur during the school year (Form A.4). These forms need to be kept in a secure location that is easily accessible for teacher or paraprofessional reference.

Common Injuries and Illnesses: Definitions and Treatments

Following are some of the most common injuries and illnesses a special education teacher is likely to encounter in the classroom, as well as a brief overview of the best course of treatment.

Abrasion

Definition   An injury consisting of the loss of a partial thickness of skin from rubbing or scraping on a hard, rough surface: also called a brush burn or friction burn (p. 268).

Treatment/Response

1.   Remove all debris.
2.   Wash away from wound with soap and water (p. 68).

Allergic Reaction

Definition   A local or general reaction to an allergen, usually characterized by hives, tissue swelling, or dyspnea (p. 268).

Treatment/Response

1.   Seek medical attention.
2.   Call parents.

Asthma

Definition   A condition marked by recurrent attacks of dyspnea with wheezing, due to spasmodic constriction of the bronchi, often as a response to allergens or to mucous plugs in the bronchioles (p. 269).

Treatment/Response

1. Comfort and reassure victim because emotional stress can make the condition worse.

2. Many asthmatics carry tablets or inhalers that relax bronchial spasms. Help them to use these medicines (p. 195).

3. Help the victim into a comfortable breathing position that he or she chooses. The best position is usually sitting upright.

4. Place the victim in a room that is as free as possible of common offenders (for example, dust, feather, animals). It should also be free of odors (for example, tobacco smoke and paint).

5. Keep conversations with asthmatics brief because they are struggling to breathe.

6. Increase the drinking of water if possible.

Seek medical attention for

- Severe, prolonged asthma attacks
- Reactions happening after an insect sting or contact with another source that produces an allergic reaction, which could progress to anaphylactic shock
- Failure to improve with medication
- Breathing that can barely be heard
- Increasing bluish skin color
- Pulse rate of more than 120 beats per minute.

Diabetes Mellitus

Definition A systemic disease marked by lack of production of insulin, which causes an inability to metabolize carbohydrates, resulting in an increase in blood sugar (p. 271).

Low Blood Sugar Symptoms

- Sudden onset
- Staggering, poor coordination
- Anger, bad temper
- Pale color
- Confusion, disorientation
- Sudden hunger
- Sweating
- Eventual stupor or unconsciousness (p. 193)

Treatment/Response

1. Provide sugar.

2. If the person can swallow without choking, offer any food or drink containing sugar, such as soft drinks, fruit juice, or candy. Do not use diet drinks when blood sugar is low.

3. If the person does not respond in 10 to 15 minutes, take him or her to the hospital (p. 193).

High Blood Sugar Symptoms

- Gradual Onset
- Drowsiness
- Extreme thirst
- Very frequent urination
- Flushed skin
- Vomiting
- Fruity or wine-like breath odor
- Heavy breathing
- Eventual stupor or unconsciousness

Action to Take

1. Take this person to the hospital.

2. If you are uncertain whether the person is suffering from high or low blood sugar, give some sugar-containing food or drink. If there is no response in 10-15 minutes, this person needs immediate medical attention.

Heat Cramps

Definition   A painful muscle cramp resulting from excessive loss of salt and water through sweating (p. 272).

Treatment/Response

1. Move the victim to a cool place.

2. Rest the cramping muscle.

3. Give victim a lot of cold water.

4. Do not massage—it rarely provides relief and may even worsen the pain (p. 162).

Heat Exhaustion

Definition   A prostration caused by excessive loss of water and salt through sweating; characterized by clammy skin and a weak, rapid pulse (p. 272).

Treatment/Response

1. Move the victim to a cool place.

2. Keep victim lying down with straight legs elevated 8-12 inches.

3. Cool the victim by applying cold packs or wet towels or cloths. Fan the victim.

4. Give the victim cold water if he or she is fully conscious.

5. If no improvement is noted within 30 minutes, seek medical attention (p. 162).

Nosebleed

Treatment/Response

Note: The authors have only included the first three of the steps recommended by the National Safety Council (p. 85).

1. Reassure and keep the victim quiet. Though a large amount of blood may appear to have been lost, most nosebleeds are not serious.

2. Keep the victim in a sitting position to reduce blood pressure.

3. Keep the victim's head tilted slightly forward so the blood can run out the front of the nose, not down the back of the throat, which causes either choking or nausea and vomiting. (The vomit could be inhaled into lungs.)

4. Accompany the student to the office or school nurse as soon as possible for further assistance.

Human Bites

Treatment/Response

1. Thoroughly wash the wound with soap and water.

2. Apply a dry, sterile dressing and seek medical attention (p. 75).

Seizure

Definition   A sudden attack or recurrence of a disease; a convulsion; an attack of epilepsy (p. 275).

Generalized Tonic-Clonic *(also called Grand Mal)*   Sudden cry, fall, rigidity, followed by muscle jerks, shallow breathing or temporarily suspended breathing, bluish skin, possible loss of bladder or bowel control, usually lasts a couple of minutes. Normal breathing then starts again. There may be some confusion and/or fatigue, followed by return to full consciousness (p. 193).

What to Do: Look for medical identification. Protect from nearby hazards. Loosen tie or shirt collars. Protect head from injury. Turn on side to keep airway clear. Reassure when consciousness returns. If single seizure lasted less than 5 minutes, ask if hospital evaluation is wanted. If multiple seizures, or if one seizure lasted longer than five minutes, call an ambulance. If person is pregnant, injured or diabetic, call for aid at once.

What Not To Do: Don't put any hard implement in the mouth. Don't try to hold tongue. It can't be swallowed. Don't try to give liquids during or just after seizure. Don't use artificial respiration unless breathing is absent after muscle jerks subside, or unless water has been inhaled. Don't restrain.

Absence *(also called Petit Mal)*   A blank stare, lasting only a few seconds, most common in children. May be accompanied by rapid blinking, some chewing movements of the mouth. Child is unaware of what's going on during the seizure, but quickly returns to full awareness once it has stopped. May result in learning difficulties if not recognized and treated (p. 193).

What to Do: No first aid necessary, but if this is the first observation of the seizure(s), medical evaluation should be recommended (p. 193).

First Aid Supplies

- Adhesive strip bandages, assorted sizes
- Adhesive tape, 1- and 2-inch rolls
- Antibiotic skin ointment
- Chemical ice pack
- Cotton balls
- Disposable latex gloves
- Elastic bandages, 2-, 3-, and 4-inch widths

- Gauze pads, 2×2 and 4×4
- Hydrogen peroxide
- Non-adhering dressing
- Scissors
- Tweezers
- Hand cleaner
- Antiseptic wipes
- Cotton swabs

Appendix A: Supplemental Forms

Form A.1   Medical history

School year: _____

Student name: _____   Date of birth: _____

Disability: _____   Grade: _____

Home telephone number: _____

Mother's work telephone number: _____
E-mail address: _____
Beeper number: _____

Father's work telephone number: _____
E-mail address: _____
Beeper number: _____

Emergency contact:

_____

Name   Relationship   Telephone number

Student's medical problem (please be specific):

_____

_____

_____

Current medication (dosage and time of administration):

_____

_____

Allergies:

_____

_____

Parent signature: _____   Date: _____

_____

Shelton, C. F., and Pollingue, A. B. *The Exceptional Teacher's Handbook: The First-Year Special Education Teacher's Guide for Success.* ©2000. Corwin Press, Inc.

Form A.2 Emergency medical plan

_____

Classroom Detention

Student: _____

Grade: _____

Date and time of detention: _____

Teacher assigning detention: _____

Reason for detention:

_____

_____

_____

_____

Parent signature: _____

Shelton, C. F., and Pollingue, A. B. *The Exceptional Teacher's Handbook: The First-Year Special Education Teacher's Guide for Success.* ©2000. Corwin Press, Inc.

Form A.3   Medical incident report

Date: _____

Student name: _____   Grade: _____

Accident or illness description:

_____

_____

_____

_____

_____

_____

_____

_____

_____

_____

_____

Teacher or paraprofessional response:

_____

_____

_____

_____

_____

_____

_____

_____

_____

_____

_____

_____

Parent or parents notified: _____ Yes or _____ No

Teacher's signature: _____

Shelton, C. F., and Pollingue, A. B. *The Exceptional Teacher's Handbook: The First-Year Special Education Teacher's Guide for Success.* ©2000. Corwin Press, Inc.

Form A.4 Medical incident report record

Date	Student Name	Discription of Injury or Illness	Teacher's Response

B

Stress Management for the Special Education Teacher

Stress Management for the New Special Education Teacher

The first-year teacher will discover very quickly that the profession of special education can be both physically and emotionally demanding. Stress is a fact of life for most special education teachers. The enormous caseloads, continual documentation of student progress, meeting the emotional and academic needs of students, and the threat of litigation are some of the contributing factors to the job-related stress experienced by new special education teachers. Although not all stress is negative, stress that impedes the teacher's ability to function in the classroom and effectively serve students is counterproductive. The authors feel that if the new teacher experiences prolonged elevated levels of job-related stress, the result could be job burnout.

The teacher must be able to effectively manage workplace stress in order to survive the entire school year. The first step in stress management is the identification of the sources of work-related stress. The following are a few of the sources identified by Zunker (1994) that the authors found to be most applicable to the special education teaching profession:

- Conditions of work (unpleasant work environment, necessity to work fast, excessive and inconvenient hours)

- Work itself (perception of job as uninteresting, repetitious, overloaded, and demanding)

- Supervision (unclear job demands, close supervision with no autonomy, scant feedback from supervisors)

- Role ambiguity (lack of clarity about one's job and scope of responsibilities)

- Group stressor (insufficient group cohesiveness, poor group identity in the organization)

- Organizational structure (too bureaucratic or too autocratic)

After the special education teacher identifies his or her stress source, the teacher must find and implement effective stress management strategies. The authors found the following techniques developed by the Georgia Association of Educators (1998) to be extremely helpful:

- Exercise
- Leave your teaching at school
- Don't schedule all of your leisure time
- Pursue a project or hobby
- Find a friend
- Don't procrastinate
- Don't feel that you must do everything
- Keep a "things to do" list
- Recognize and accept your limitations
- Learn to tolerate and forgive
- Learn to plan
- Be a positive person
- Learn to play
- Rid yourself of worry

Finally, if the new special education teacher continues to have difficulty with stress management, the authors suggest that the teacher enroll in staff development courses designed to teach stress management strategies to school employees. In addition, the teacher should contact his or her school administrator or special education director if all attempts at stress reduction have failed.

Organizations for Parents of Exceptional Students

Family Resource Center on Disabilities (FRCD)
   c/o Charlotte Des Jardins
   20 East Jackson Blvd., RM 900
   Chicago, IL 60604
   Charlotte Des Jardins, Executive Director
   Telephone: (312) 939-3513
   Toll-free: (800) 952-4199
   Fax: (312) 939-7297

Beach Center on Families and Disability
   c/o Ann Turnbull
   3111 Haworth Hall
   Lawrence, KS 66045
   Ann Turnbull, codirector
   Telephone: (913) 864-7600
   Fax: (913) 864-7605
   E-mail: **beach@dole.isu.ukans.edu**

Center on Human Policy
   805 S. Crouse Ave.
   Syracuse, NY 13244-2280
   Steven Taylor Ph.D., Director
   Telephone: (315) 443-3851
   Toll-free: (800) 894-0826
   Fax: (315) 443-4338
   E-mail: **thehp@sued.syr.edu**

Clearing House on Disability Information (CDI)
   United States Department of Education
   Office of Special Education and Rehabilitative Services
   Switzer Building, RM 3132
   Washington, DC 20202-2524
   Telephone: (202) 205-8241
   Fax: (202) 205-9252

Disabled and Alone: Life Services for the Handicapped
  c/o Leslie D. Park
  352 Park Avenue S., Ste. 703
  New York, NY 10010
  Leslie D. Park, Chairman
  Telephone: (212) 532-6740
  (212) 532-3588
  Toll-free: (800) 995-0066
  Fax: (212) 532-6740

Goodwill Industries International (GII)
  9200 Wisconsin Avenue
  Bethesda, MD 20814
  Fred Grandy, President and CEO
  Telephone: (301) 530-6500
  Fax: (301) 530-1516

National Information Center for Children and Youth with Disabilities
  (NICHCY)
  PO Box 1492
  Washington, DC 20013
  Suzanne Ripley, Director
  Telephone: (202) 884-8200
  Toll-free: (800) 695-0285
  Fax: (202) 884-8441
  E-mail: **nichcy@aed.org**.

Sibling Information Network
  c/o University of Connecticut
  249 Glenbrook Road
  Box U-64
  Storrs Mansfield, CT 06268
  Lisa Glidden, coordinator
  Telephone: (203) 486-5035
  (203) 486-4985
  Fax: (203) 486-5037
  E-mail: **speadm01@uconn.umucenn.edu**

Web Sites

Alliance of Genetic Support Groups: Provides a list of support groups pertaining to particular genetic conditions.

  www.geneticalliance.org

The Arc: A National Organization on Mental Retardation.

  http://TheArc.org/

Family Village: A global community that integrates information, resources, and communication opportunities on the Internet for persons with disabilities, their families, and those who provide services.

www.familyvillage.wisc.edu/

Federation for Children with Special Needs: A center for parents and parent organizations to work together on behalf of children with special needs and their families.

www.fcsn.org/

Federation of Families for Children Mental Health: Making a difference in the lives of children with EBD or mental disorders.

www.ffcmh.org

Internet Resources for Special Children (IRSC): Provides parents, educators, medical professionals, and caregivers with information regarding children with disabilities.

www.irsc.org

LD Association of America:

www.ldantl.org

On-line Support Groups: A list of on-line support groups under general topic headings.

http://disabilities.about.com/health/disabilities

Parents/Professional for Exceptional Problems: A coalition of parents and medical professionals providing information on all treatments and the care for children who are sensory challenged.

www.pepe-usa.org/

Sympatico/Healthway: Provides information on a variety of health and disability topics.

http://www.nt.sympaticao.ca/healthway/health.html

Organizations for Exceptional Students

Learning Disabilities Special Interest Group (LDSIG)
Westork College
PO Box 3649
Fort Smith, AR 72903
Zanette Douglas, Contact
Telephone: (501) 788-7667

Accent on Information (AOI)
PO Box 700
Bloomington, IL 61702
Betty Garee, editor
Telephone: (309) 378-2961
Fax: (307) 378-4420
E-mail: **cheeverpub@aol.com**

Advocates for Communication Technology for Deaf/Blind People (ACT)
PO Box 652
Columbia, MID 21045
Telephone: (410) 381-3377

American Amputee Foundation (AAF)
Box 250218, Hillcrest Station
Little Rock AR 72225
Jack M. East, Executive Director
Telephone: (501) 666-2523
(501) 666-9540
Fax: (501) 666-83695)

American Association of People with Disabilities (AAPD)
1819 H. Street NWE, Ste. 330
Washington, DC 20006
Web site: **http://www.aapd.com/**
Telephone: (202) 457-8168
Toll-free: (800) 840-8844
Fax: (202) 457-0473

Assistance Dogs of America (ADAI)
    8806 State Rte. 64
    Swanton, OH 43558
    Dino Brownson, President
    Telephone: (419) 825-3622
    Toll-free: (800) 841-2254
    Web site: **http://www.adai.org.**

Council of Citizens with Low Vision (CCLV)
    1400 N. Drake Road, No. 218
    Kalamazoo, MI 49006
    Elizabeth Lennon, Liaison
    Telephone: (616) 381- 9566
    Toll-free: 800-733-2258

Direct Link for the Disabled
    c/o Linda Lee Harry
    PO Box 1464
    Solvang, CA 93464-1464
    Telephone: (805) 688-1603
    (805) 686-5384
    Fax: (805) 686-5285
    E-mail: **suharry@terminus.com**

Just One Break (JOB)
    120 Wall Street
    New York, NY 10005
    Mikki Lam, Executive Director
    Telephone: (212) 785-7300
    Fax: (212) 785-4513

National Center for Youth with Disabilities (NCYD)
    University of Minnesota
    Division of General Pediatrics and Adolescent Health
    Box 721
    420 Delaware Street SE
    Minneapolis, MN 55455
    Telephone: (612) 626-2825
    Fax: (612) 626-2134
    E-mail: **neyd@gold.tc.umn.edu**

Web Sites

Ability Online Support Network: An electronic mail forum providing support for children and young adults with disabilities and chronic illness that helps build self-esteem by eliminating barriers between disabled kids and their non-disabled peers.

    www.able.link.org

Family Voices:

www.familyvoices.org

Foundation for Exceptional Children:

www.cec.sped.org/fd/back.html

National Coalition for Student with Disabilities:

www.essential.org

The Sibling Support Group: Dedicated to the interest of brothers and sisters of people with special health and developmental needs.

www.chmc.org/departmt/sibsupp/

World Institute on Disabilities: Dedicated to the promotion of independence and full inclusion in society of people with disabilities.

www.wid.org

E

Guide to Locating
Instructional Materials

Academic Communication Associates, Inc.
    Publication Center, Dept. 62E
    4149 Avenida de la Plata
    PO Box 4279
    Oceanside, CA 92052-4279
    Telephone: (760) 758-9593
    Fax: (760) 758-1604

Academic Therapy Publications
    20 Commercial Boulevard
    Novato, CA 94949-6191
    Telephone: (415) 883-3314
    Fax: (415) 883-3720
    Web site: **http://www.atpub.com**

Addison Wesley Longman Publishing Co.
    1 Jacob Way
    Reading, MA 01867
    Telephone: 800-552-2499
    Fax: (800) 284-8292
    Web site: **http://www.awl.com**

ADD Warehouse
    300 NW 70th Avenue, Suite 102
    Plantation, FL 333317
    Telephone: 800-233-9273
    Fax: (954) 792-8545
    Web site: **www.addwarehouse.com**

American Guidance Service—AGS
    4201 Woodland Road
    Circle Pines, MN 55014-1796
    Telephone: (800) 328-2560
    Fax: (612) 786-9077
    Web site: **www.agsnet.com**

Attainment Company
   PO Box
   Verona, WI 53593-0160
   Telephone: (800) 327-4269
   Fax: (800) 942-3865

Bureau for At-Risk Youth
   135 Dupont Street
   PO Box 760
   Plainview, NY 11803-0760
   Telephone: (800) 999-6884
   Fax: (516) 349-5521
   Web site: **www.at-risk.com**

C. H. Stoelting Co.
   620 Wheat Lane
   Wood Dale, IL 60191
   Telephone: (630) 860-9700
   Fax: (630) 860-9775
   Web site: **www.stoeltingco.com/tests**

Cambridge Development Laboratory, Inc.
   86 West Street
   Waltham, MA 02451
   Telephone: (800) 637-0047
   Fax: (781) 890-2894
   Web site: **www.cdlspecial.com**

Capstone Curriculum Publishing
   151 Good Counsel Drive
   PO Box 669
   Mankato, MN 56002-0669
   Telephone: (888) 574-6711
   Fax: (888) 574-6183

Center on Education and Work
   University of Wisconsin-Madison
   School of Education
   964 Educational Sciences Building
   1025 W. Johnson Street
   Madison, WI 53706-1796
   Telephone: (800) 446-0399
   Fax: (608) 262-9197
   Web site: **www.cew.wise.edu**

Channing L. Bete Co., Inc.
   200 State Road
   South Deerfield, MA 01373-0200
   Telephone: (800) 628-7733
   Fax: (800) 499-6464

Child's Work Child's PLAY
   Genesis Direct Inc.
   100 Plaza Drive
   Secaucus, NJ 07094-3613
   Telephone: (800) 962-1141
   Fax: (201) 583-3644
   Web site: **www.childsplay.com**

Corwin Press, Inc.
   2455 Teller Road
   Thousand Oaks, CA 91320-2218
   Telephone: (805) 499-9774
   Fax: (800) 417-2466
   Web site: **www.corwinpress.com**

Curriculum Associates
   5 Esquire Road, N
   Billerica, MA 01862-2589
   Telephone: (800) 225-0248
   Fax: (800) 366-1158
   Web site: **www.curriculumassociates.com**

EBSCO Curriculum Materials
   Box 11521
   Birmingham, AL 35202-1521
   Telephone: (800) 633-8623
   Fax: (205) 991-1482
   Web site: **http://www.ecmtest.com**

Educational Design
   345 Hudson Street
   New York, NY 10014-4502
   Telephone: (800) 221-9372
   Fax: (212) 675-6922
   Web site: **www.educationaldesign.com**

Educators Publishing Service, Inc.
   31 Smith Place
   Cambridge, MA 02138
   Telephone: (800) 225-5750
   Fax: (617) 547-0412
   Web site: **www.epsbooks.com**

Funtastic Therapy
   RD 4 Box 14, John White Road
   Cranberry, NJ 08512
   Telephone: (800) 531-3176
   Fax: (609) 275-0488

Glencoe/McGraw-Hill
　　PO Box 508
　　Columbus, OH 43216
　　Telephone: (800) 334-7344
　　Fax: (614) 860-1877
　　Web site: **http://www.glencoe.com**

Globe Fearon Publishers
　　4350 Equity Drive
　　PO Box 2649
　　Columbus, OH 43216
　　Telephone: (800) 848-9500
　　Fax: (614) 771-7361

Greenwood Publishing Group, Inc.
　　88 Post Road West
　　Westport, CT 06881
　　Telephone: (203) 226-3571
　　Fax: (203) 222-1502
　　Web site: **http://www.greenwood.com**

Hawthorne Educational Services
　　800 Gray Oak Drive
　　Columbia, MO 65201
　　Telephone: (800) 542-1673
　　Fax: (800) 442-9509

Huby's Ltd.
　　School to Work Catalog
　　Department: W99
　　PO Box 9117
　　Jackson, WY 83002
　　Telephone: (800) 543-0998
　　Fax: (800) 518-2514

J. Weston Walch Publishers
　　321 Valley Street
　　PO Box 658
　　Portland, Maine 04104-0658
　　Telephone: (800) 341-6094
　　Fax: (207) 772-3105

Kaplan Concepts for Exceptional Children
　　PO Box 609
　　1310 Lewisville-Clemmons Road
　　Lewisville, NC 27023-0609
　　Telephone: (800) 334-2014
　　Fax: (800) 452-7526
　　Web site: **http://www.kaplanco.com**

Lakeshore Learning Materials
2695 East Dominquez Street
PO Box 6261
Carson, CA 90749
Telephone: (800) 421-5354
Fax: (310) 537-5403
Web site: **http://www.lakeshorelearning.com**

PCI Educational Publishing
2800 NE Loop 410, Suite 105
San Antonio, Texas 78218-1525
Telephone: (800) 594-4263
Fax: (888) 259-8284
Web site: **http://www.pcicatalog.com**

Prufrock Press
PO Box 8813
Waco, TX 76714-8813
Telephone: (800) 998-2208
FAX: (800) 240-0333
Web site: **http://www.prufrock.com/**

Remedia Publications
10135 East Via Linda, Suite D124
Scottsdale, AZ 85258-5312
Telephone: (800) 826-4740
Fax: (602) 661-9901
Web site: **http://www.rempub.com**

Research Press
PO Box 9177
Champaign, IL 61826
Telephone: (800) 510-2707
Fax: (217) 252-1221
Web site: **http://www.researchpress.com**

Resources for Educators
PO Box 362916
Des Moines, IA 50336-2916
Telephone: (800) 491-0551
Fax: (800) 835-5327
Web site: **http://www.phdirect.com**

Saddleback Educational, Inc.
    3503 Cadillac Avenue, Building F-9
    Costa Mesa, CA 92618-2767
    Telephone: (949) 860-2500
    Fax: (949) 860-2508

Scholastic, Inc.
    PO Box 7502
    Jefferson City, MO 65102
    Telephone: (800) 724-6527
    Fax: (573) 635-7630

Scott Foresman/Addison Wesley
    School Services
    1 Jacob Way
    Reading, MA 01867
    Telephone: (800) 552-2259
    Fax: (800) 333-3328
    Web site: **http://www.sf.aw.com**

Slosson
    PO Box 280
    East Aurora, NY 14052-0280
    Telephone: (888) 756-7766
    Fax: (800) 655-3840
    Web site: **http://www.slosson.com**

SRA/McGraw-Hill
    220 East Danieldale Road
    DeSoto, TX 75115-2490
    Telephone: (800) 843-8855
    Fax: (214) 228-1982
    Web site: **http://www.sra-4kids.com**

Teacher Ideas Press
    PO Box 6633
    Englewood, CO 80155-6633
    Telephone: (800) 237-6124
    Fax: (303) 220-8843
    Web site: **http://www.lu.com**

Things for Learning
    PO Box 908
    Rutherfordton, NC 28139
    Telephone: (800) 228-6178
    Fax: (704) 287-9506

Pharmacology Reference List

Important Note: The pharmacology information contained in this section is intended to serve only as a reference source for the first-year special education teacher and not treatment recommendations by the authors. The new teacher should consult a medical professional or school psychologist with questions or concerns pertaining to a particular drug therapy.

Table F.1   Depression

Brand Name*	Generic Name**	Usual Daily Dose (Mg)**
Elavil, Endep	amitryptyline	75–150
Asendin	amoxapine	200–300
Norpramin, Pertofrane	desipramine	75–200
Adapin, Sinequan	doxepin	75–150
Prozac	fluoxetine	20–80
Janimine, SK-Pramine, Tofranil	imipramine	50–200
Marplan	isocarboxazid	10–30
Ludiomil	maprotiline	75–150
Aventyl, Pamelor	nortriphyline	75–100
Nardil	phenelzine	15–30
Vivactil	protriptyline	15–40
Parnate	tranylcypromine	20–30
Desyrel	trazodone	150–600

*Adapted from Poling, Gadow, and Cleary, 1991, pp. 149–152.
**Adapted from Lickey and Gordon, 1991, pp. 380–382.
***Adapted from Sifton, 1996, pp. 145–581.

Table F.2   Anxiety

Brand Name*	Generic Name**	Usual Daily Dosage (Mg)**
Xanax	Alprozolam	0.75–1.5
BuSpar	Buspirone	15–30
Librium	Chloridazeproxide	15–40
Tranxene	Clorazepate	30
Valium	Diazepam	4–40
Paxipam	Halazepam	60–160
Ativan	Lorazepam	2–6
Miltown, Equanil	meprobamate	1,200–1,600
Serax	Oxazepan	30–60
Centrax	Prazepam	20–40

*Adapted from Poling, Gadow, and Cleary, 1991, pp. 149–152.
**Adapted from Lickey and Gordon, 1991, pp. 380–382.
***Adapted from Sifton, 1996, pp. 145–581.

Table F.3   Attention deficit disorder, attention deficit hyperactivity disorder

Brand Name*	Generic Name**	Usual Daily Dosage (Mg)***
Ritalin	Methylphenidate	5–60
Cylert	Pemoline	56.25–75
Dexedrine	Dextroamphetamine	2.5–40

*Adapted from Poling, Gadow, and Cleary, 1991, pp. 149–152.
**Adapted from Lickey and Gordon, 1991, pp. 380–382.
***Adapted from Sifton, 1996, pp. 145–581.

Table F.4   Epilepsy

Brand Name*	Generic Name**	Usual Daily Dosage (Mg)***
Diamox	Acetazolamide	8–30 milligrams
Tegretol	Carbamazepine	400–800
Klonopin	Clonazepam	0.01–0.2 milligram
Valium	diazepam	1–2.5
Dilantin	Diphenylhydantoin	5–300
Mysoline	Primidone	125–250

*Adapted from Poling, Gadow, and Cleary, 1991, pp. 149—152.
**Adapted from Lickey and Gordon, 1991, pp. 380—382.
***Adapted from Sifton, 1996, pp. 145—581.

References

References Chapter 2

Gearheart, B. R., Mullen, R. C., and Gearheart, C. J. *Exceptional Individuals: An Introduction.* Belmont, California: Wadsworth, Inc., 1993.

Grossman, H. J. (ed.). *Classification in Mental Retardation.* Washington, DC: American Association on Mental Deficiency, 1983.

Individuals with Disabilities Education Act of 1975, Pub. L. No. 105-17, *Federal Register, Vol. 64,* No. 48, 1999.

Schildroth, A. N., and Karchmer, M. A. *Deaf Children in America.* Austin, TX: Pro-Ed, 1986.

Smith, D. D., and Luckasson, R. *Introduction to Special Education Teaching in the Age of Challenge.* Needham Heights, MA: Allyn and Bacon, 1992.

References Chapter 3

Arlington County Public Schools. Testing and evaluation tips. In *LD On-Line: Testing and Evaluation Tips* (online) 1999. Available at http://www.ldonline_indepth/teaching_techniques/testin_ tips.html

Rizzo, J. V., and Zabel, R. H. *Educating Children and Adolescents with Behavioral Disorders: An Integrative Approach.* Needham Heights, MA: Allyn and Bacon, Inc., 1988.

Roberts, J. *Classroom Management for ADD/ADHD Students (and Other Behavioral Problems).* In *Teachers Helping Teachers* (online) 1999. Available: http://www.pacific-net.net/~mandel/SpecialEducation.html

Shea, I. M., and Bauer, A. M. *Parents and Teachers of Children with Exceptionalities.* Needham Heights, MA: Allyn and Bacon, 1991.

Smith, D. D., and Luckasson, R. *Introduction to Special Education Teaching in the Age of Challenge.* Needham Heights, MA: Allyn and Bacon, 1992.

The Office of Disability Resources. *Guidelines to Classroom Modifications for Students with Disabilities.* In Bowling Green State University Disability Services [On-line]. Available: http://www.bgsu.edu/offices/student_affairs/general/modifications/modifications.html

References Chapter 4

Koorland, M. "The Behavior Analysis Model." In *Solving Discipline Problems: Methods and Models for Today's Teachers,* 1995, p. 149.

Canter, L., and Canter, M. "Assertive Discipline." In *Solving Discipline Problems: Methods and Models For Today's Teachers,* 1995, p. 255.

Wolfgang, C. H. *Solving Discipline Problems: Methods and Models for Today's Teachers.* Needham Heights, MA: Simon and Schuster, 1995.

Wong, H. *The Effective Teacher.* Sunnyvale, CA: Wong Publications, 1991.

References Chapter 5

Mercer, C. D., and Mercer, A. R. *Teaching Students with Learning Problems.* New York: Macmillan Publishing Group, 1993.

References Chapter 6

Kroth, R. L., and Simpson, R. L. *Parent Conferences: A Teaching Strategy.* Denver, CO: Love, 1977.

Shea, T. M., and Bauer, A. M. *Parents and Teachers of Children with Exceptionalities.* Needham Heights, MA: Allyn and Bacon, 1991.

References Chapter 7

Canter, A. *Understanding Test Scores: A Handout for Teachers.* National Association of School Psychologists, pp. 119-120, 1998.

Linn, J. E., and Gronlund, M. A. *Measurement and Assessment in Teaching.* Englewood Cliffs, NJ: Prentice-Hall, Inc., 1995.

Mehrens, W. A., and Lehmann, I. J. *Using Standardized Tests in Education.* White Plains, NY: Longman Inc., 1987.

Sweetland, R. C., and O'Connor, William (eds.). *Tests: A Comprehensive Reference for Assessments in Psychology, Education, and Business.* Kansas City, MO: SKS Associates, 1984.

References Chapter 8

Individuals with Disabilities Education Act of 1975, Pub L. No. 105–117, *Federal Register, Vol. 64,* No. 48, 1999.

Mager, R. F. *Preparing Instructional Objectives.* Belmont, CA: Pitman Learning, Inc., 1984.

References Chapter 9

CEC Today. *A Primer on IDEA and Its Regulations.* 5 (7), 5, 1999.

Mastropieri, M., and Scruggs, T. *The Inclusive Classroom: Strategies for Effective Instruction.* Columbus, OH: Merrill, 2000.

Wehman, P. *Life Beyond the Classroom* (2nd ed.) Baltimore, MD: Brookes, 1996.

References Appendix A

National Safety Council. *First Aid and CPR* (2nd ed.) Boston: Jones and Bartlett, 1992.

References Appendix B

Georgia Association of Educators. *Avoiding Burnout and Staying Healthy* [On-line] 1998. Available at http://www.gae.org/teacher/te_burnout.html

Zunker, V. G. *Career Counseling: Applied Concepts of Life Planning* (4th ed.) Pacific Grove, CA: Brooks/Cole Publishing Company, 1994.

References Appendix F

Lickey, M. E., and Gordon, B. *Medicine and Mental Illness: The Use of Drugs in Psychiatry.* USA: W. H. Freeman and Company, 1991.

Poling, A., Gadow, K., and Cleary, J. *Drug Therapy for Behavior Disorders: An Introduction.* Elmsford, New York: Pergamon Press, 1991.

Sifton, D., Larbi, A., Kelly, G., and Perin, T. *The PRD Family Guide to Prescription Drugs* (4th ed.) Montvale, NJ: Medical Economics Company, Inc., 1996.

CORWIN
PRESS